The Random Book of…

RICHARD

Richard Shanahan

The Random Book of…

RICHARD

Well, I didn't know that!

All statistics, facts and figures are correct as of March 31st 2009.

Published By:

Stripe Publishing Ltd
First Floor, 3 St. Georges Place, Brighton, BN1 4GA

Email: info@stripepublishing.co.uk
Web: www.stripepublishing.co.uk

First published 2009

10-digit ISBN: 1-907158-08-1
13-digit ISBN: 978-1-907158-08-7

Printed and bound by Gutenberg Press Ltd., Malta.

Editor: Dan Tester
Illustrations: Jonathan Pugh (www.pughcartoons.co.uk)
Typesetting: Andrew Searle
Cover: Andy Heath

INTRODUCTION

When I was asked to write this book I was immediately enthusiastic.

I have always found it interesting and satisfying to learn about people with whom I share my name. Then I was a little worried that I would not be able to find enough Richards to fill a book even as small as this.

As I researched Richards and talked to friends and family about the project I quickly found that I would run out of space. And then the question became who to leave out.

I am a musician and a natural curiosity to discover fellow musical Richards meant that I found enough of us to write a book entirely about Richards in the music business.

However, variety is the spice of life and in the following pages the reader will find all sorts of Richards rubbing shoulders; kings and a president; cricketers, footballers and Olympic medallists; artists, writers and musicians and madmen and saints all vie to tell us their stories.

But, there are still many more Richards shaking their heads in disappointment at not being included.

And just maybe one of the Richards reading this will be eager to make the next edition...

THE RANDOM BOOK OF... RICHARD

A Germanic name, derived from the words 'ric' (ruler, rich) and 'hard' (strong, brave) Richard originally meant strong king.

Two early French Dukes, Richard, Comte de Rouen, born between 760 and 765, and Richard Graf von Amiens, born about 785 and died about 825, represent the earliest examples of the name in history.

The name was introduced to England by the Normans and was fashionable amongst the early royal families. The Plantagenet dynasty named six of their sons, three of whom were kings, Richard. After the death of Richard III, the last of the Yorks, the name declined until the 18th century when it became popular again.

According to census data, 4,671 babies were named Richard in 1807 but that fell to 2,289 in 1907. Only 538 babies named Richard were registered in 2005.

Time to re-start the popularity campaign!

Between the 1920s and 1970s Richard was ever-present in the top ten most popular boy's names in the United States and regularly rose as high as fifth.

There are many translations and diminutives of Richard:

Alternatives: **Ricard, Richarde, Richaud, Rychard**

Basque:	**Edrigu**
Finnish:	**Rikkard**
German:	**Rikert, Rickert, Rheinhard**
Hungarian:	**Rikard**
Irish:	**Ristéard**
Italian:	**Riccardo**
Latin:	**Ricardus, Richardus**
Polish:	**Ryszard**
Portuguese:	**Ricardo**
Scandinavian:	**Rikard**
Spanish:	**Ricardo**
Swedish:	**Rikard**
Welsh:	**Rhisiart**

<u>Diminutives</u>:

Cornish:	**Hicca**
English:	**Diccon, Dick, Dickie, Dickon, Digg, Hick, Higg, Hitch, Hitchcock, Rich, Ritchie, Rick, Rickey, Ricky**
Hawaiian:	**Lika, Liki**
Spanish:	**Rico**

Richard is also used as a surname, as are variations Richards and Richardson.

Richenda, an 18th century name, is the female version of Richard. **Richenda Carey** is a British television, film and theatre actress. She has appeared in BBC's *Monarch of the Glen* and the film *Lara Croft: Tomb Raider* (2001).

Richildis is an early Norman woman's name which is also a feminised variant of Richard.

According to the Urban Dictionary 'A Richard could have been born to the Earth to change it, to revolutionise, to excel and leave his mark upon the world.'

And it can also be used as 'a general expression of negativity, especially disappointment.'

Normally, Richard is only used to refer to others' actions and the results of such actions. It may stand in place of 'dick', but proper usage does not require this to be so.

It is frequently prefaced by an intensifier, such as 'extremely', for example "a friend does something untoward, like stealing the chips that you really wanted. You notify him: 'That was a Richard move, man.'

A party is filled with undesirable company. You note: 'This party is really Richard.'

Saint Richard of Chichester (also known as **Richard de Wych**) is a saint (canonized 1262) who was Bishop of Chichester. His shrine in Chichester Cathedral was a richly-decorated centre of pilgrimage which was destroyed in 1538.

Saint Richard is best remembered today for the popular prayer ascribed to him as his last words on his deathbed where, surrounded by the clergy of his diocese, he prayed:

Thanks be to Thee, my Lord Jesus Christ
For all the benefits Thou hast given me,
For all the pains and insults Thou hast borne for me.
O most merciful Redeemer, friend and brother,
May I know Thee more clearly,
Love Thee more dearly,
Follow Thee more nearly,
Day by day.

This prayer was adapted for the song 'Day by Day' in the musical *Godspell*.

FICTIONAL RICHARDS

Bernard Cornwell's fictional **Richard Sharpe** is the central character in more than 20 historical novels. A hero of the Napoleonic Wars, Sharpe is played in ITV's costume dramas by Sean Bean.

Dick Grayson first appeared as Batman's crime fighting sidekick Robin in April 1940. The Boy Wonder was played in the 1960s TV series by Burt Ward and in *Batman Forever* (1995) and *Batman and Robin* (1997) by Chris O'Donnell.

Dick Barton-Special Agent was a popular radio show on the BBC's Light Programme. The serial aired daily from 1946 to 1951 and, at its peak, had an audience of 15 million. The show was killed off to make way for *The Archers*.

Richie Cunningham was a star of 1970s hit sitcom *Happy Days* (1974-84). Played by the now successful film director Ron Howard, Cunningham was the wholesome all-American high school kid who was friends with The Fonz, Potsie and Ralph Malph.

David Janssen was *The Fugitive* (1963-67), **Richard Kimble**, for four seasons and 120 episodes. Wrongly accused of the murder of his wife, Kimble had to avoid the pursuit of his nemesis Lt. Philip Gerard and find The One Armed Man, his wife's real killer.

Kimble was played by Harrison Ford in the 1993 film version based loosely on the television series.

Major-General Sir Richard Hannay, KCB, OBE, DSO, Legion of Honour, is a fictional secret agent created by Scottish novelist John Buchan. He appears in several novels, including; *The Thirty-Nine Steps* (1915), *Greenmantle* (1916), *Mr. Standfast* (1919), *The Three Hostages* (1924), *The Courts of the Morning* (1929), *The Island of Sheep* (1936) and *Sick Heart River* (1940).

Hannay has been played by Robert Donat, Kenneth More and Robert Powell in three film versions of *The Thirty-Nine Steps* and by Orson Welles in a radio version of the novel.

Hard-hitting, fast-shooting, and supremely intelligent police detective **Dick Tracy** was created by cartoonist Chester Gould in 1931. Tracy became a major character in American popular culture appearing in radio, television and film serialisations, the most recent being his portrayal by Warren Beatty in 1990.

Richie Aprile is a fictional criminal who appeared in ten episodes of *The Sopranos*. After his release from prison Aprile threatens and menaces many of the TV show's characters. Although a hit is planned by the crime family boss, Tony Soprano, Aprile is eventually killed by his girlfriend Janice (Soprano's sister) in a domestic argument.

REAL RICHARDS

Richard Fitzalan was a Norman nobleman and the 8th Earl of Arundel. He became Earl in 1289 and, in that same year, was knighted by Edward I. He fought in the wars of the Welsh Marches between 1288 and 1294 and was himself a feudal Lord, occupying Clun and Oswestry.

The 10th Earl of Arundel was also called **Richard Fitzalan** and was nicknamed 'Copped-Hat'. Although his father was executed for plotting against Edward II, Richard managed to regain the Earldom for the Fitzalans.

He became a trusted supporter of Edward, The Black Prince, and helped his campaigns against the Welsh. In 1334 he was made Justiciar of North Wales, Sheriff for life of Caernarvonshire, and Governor of Caernarfon Castle.

He fought for the English Crown on campaigns in Scotland and in France. As a reward he was given the Earldom of Surrey in 1347, which increased his already great wealth. He was reckoned to be one of the richest men in England.

After the death of his father in 1376, **Richard Fitzalan** became the third family member with that name to bear the title Earl of Arundel. He was the 11th.

He also made his reputation as a strong military leader and in 1377 was Admiral of the West and South. By 1386 King Richard II had made him Admiral of all England and he defeated a Franco-Spanish-Flemish fleet off the coast of Margate in 1387.

In 1397 Fitzalan was arrested for his opposition to the policies of Richard II. He was beheaded on September 21st of that year and was buried at the church of the Augustin friars in Bread Street, London.

Richard, Duke of Burgundy, was a French nobleman and also known as Richard the Justiciar. His younger sister, Richildis, married Charles the Bald, who Richard accompanied on his journey to be crowned Holy Roman Emperor in 875.

He died in 921 after uniting all of the counties of Burgundy.

Born around 1045, **Richard of Salerno**, was a participant in the First Crusade of 1097. He was one of the few Crusaders who could speak Arabic due to his campaigns in the ward in Sicily, which then had a strong Moorish presence.

In 1098 he fought in the Siege of Antioch with Tancred.

After crusading he retired to Marash in present day Turkey in 1111. He was killed when the Great Earthquake shook the town in 1114.

Richard of Wallingford was a 14th century constable and landowner in St. Albans. He played a significant part in the Peasant's Revolt of 1381 and helped to organise Wat Tyler's campaign. He was present when the rebels made their demands to King Richard II. After Tyler's death many of the rebellion leaders were executed but Wallingford was imprisoned. He was later pardoned and released by the king.

An earlier **Richard of Wallingford** (1292-1336) was an Abbot of St. Albans and highly regarded by his contemporaries as a mathematician, astronomer, astrologist and horologist. He has been called one of the greatest scientists of the Middle Ages.

In 1326 he designed one of the most complex clocks of the times, a re-creation of which is on display at St. Albans Cathedral.

He later designed a calculation device (an equatorium he named Albion) which was used for lunar, solar and planetary longitudes. It could also predict eclipses.

Richard Folville was rector of a small parish church in Teigh, near Melton Mowbray in Leicestershire. Despite being appointed to the church in 1321, Richard still took part in gang activity with his six brothers.

It is thought that he was the mastermind behind the kidnapping and ransom of Chief Justice of the King's Bench, **Sir Richard Willoughby**, in 1332. The Folvilles abducted Willoughby and demanded a pay off of 1300 Marks. This was duly paid by King Edward II and Willoughby was set free after declaring loyalty to the brigands.

In 1340 or 1341, Folville was surrounded in Teigh by **Sir Richard de Coalville**, a Justice of the Peace, and after a fierce battle was drawn outside. Folville was beheaded in his own churchyard by Coalville.

In 1303, **Richard of Pudlicott,** an unlucky English wool merchant, was the brains behind an audacious robbery of the king's wardrobe at Westminster Abbey. He and his collaborators stole gems, antique gold and coins estimated at £100,000 in value (or equal to about a year's tax income).

When stolen items began flooding the market the royal court were alerted and they rounded up hundreds of suspects. While on trial Richard lied to save his accomplices – the clergy at the Abbey – from being implicated and executed. Most of the suspects were released on Pudlicott's testimony but he was hanged along with a dozen of his co-conspirators.

The de Clare family is another Norman dynasty noted for its fondness for the name Richard.

Richard FitzGilbert was the founder of the family dynasty and accompanied William the Conqueror on his invasion in 1066. He served William at the Battle of Hastings and was crucial in subduing the Anglo-Saxon resistance. He was rewarded by the new king with 176 lordships and large grants of land.

He built castles at Clare, in Suffolk, from which he took the family name, and Tonbridge.

He was made Chief Justiciar by William and played a key role in suppressing the rebellion of 1075. He died in 1090.

Richard FitzGilbert de Clare, 1st Earl of Hertford, was his grandson. He was also Lord Ceredigion and spent much of his time in the border regions in Wales. In 1136 he ignored warnings of an imminent Welsh uprising and was attacked and killed.

His son, **Richard de Clare, 2nd Earl of Pembroke**, Lord of Leinster, Justiciar of Ireland, was part of the Norman invasion force which attempted to subdue Ireland in 1170. He was nicknamed 'Strongbow', for his prowess with the longbow.

After a six year campaign in Ireland, de Clare died from an infected foot wound.

Richard de Clare, 4th Earl of Hertford was the son of Roger de Clare, 3rd Earl of Hertford. He was present at the coronations of Richard I in 1189 and John in 1199. He also played a key part in the negotiations which resulted in the Magna Carta.

Richard de Clare, 6th Earl of Hertford, died in 1262 and was the final Richard of the De Clare line.

Richard 'Galloping Dick' Ferguson was an English highwayman during the late 18th century. He formed a partnership with another notorious highwayman of the time, Jerry Abershawe.

When his father died he left Richard his life savings of £57. Rather than work Richard took up the life of a gentleman and spent his time attending theatre and society functions. He was mistaken by a courtesan for a wealthy landowner and he spent much time with her.

His money quickly ran out, however, and Ferguson was forced back to his old job. While driving his carriage through the backstreets of London he was stopped by two masked highwaymen, one of whom he recognised as an acquaintance of the courtesan he had been seeing.

The familiar man, Jerry Abershawe, gave Ferguson a bribe to keep quiet. Thereafter, Ferguson gave Abershawe tips on who to pick off on the road. The two later became accomplices.

Abershawe was caught and executed in 1795 and Ferguson maintained a successful solo career for five years, until he was caught by the Bow Street Runners in 1800 and publicly executed.

Colonel **Richard Martin** was an Irish politician of the late 18th and early 19th centuries. He was an MP in the Irish Parliament and then represented Galway at Westminster when the Irish Parliament was dissolved in 1800 by the Act of Union. He was well known for his humorous speeches and interruptions.

Martin worked hard to secure the emancipation of Irish Catholics, which was granted in 1829.

He also worked tirelessly against cruelty to animals and fought against bear baiting and dog fighting. He introduced Martin's Act to Parliament in 1822, which attempted to prevent these things.

He once challenged a man to a duel for his mistreatment of a dog. When asked why he would fight with weapons over an animal, he replied; "Sir, an ox cannot hold a pistol."

He was present when the Society for the Prevention of Cruelty to Animals (a forerunner of the present RSPCA) was formed in London in 1824 and his fondness for animals led to him being nicknamed 'Humanity Dick', by George IV. He also acquired the nickname of 'Hair trigger Dick', because of his keenness for duelling with swords and pistols. He fought over 100 of these.

Martin travelled extensively during chaotic times and was in New England when the revolutionary fervour against England was fermenting. He was also in France during the 1789 revolution.

Richard Brandon was a 17th century English hangman and executioner. He is often cited as the man who executed Charles I, by beheading, on January 30th 1649.

He was paid £30 for the job and was apparently paid his fee in half crowns. He took an orange stuck with cloves from Charles and later sold it for ten shillings in Rosemary Lane.

Dr. Richard Beeching (1913-1985) was a physicist and engineer and became the first Chairman of British Railways in March 1961. Almost everything about Beeching at the time was controversial.

He managed to secure a salary of £24,000 (£367,000 in today's money) which was higher than any other head of a nationalised industry.

Beeching is most famous as the author of *The Re-shaping of British Railways* (1963) in which he suggested massive cuts to the rail system. In his attempts to make British Rail profitable (it was running annual losses of £140 million) he pruned more than 4,000 miles from the network and predicted 70,000 job losses.

By the time he presented his second report in 1965 there was a Labour government, which rejected his proposals and he left his post under a cloud.

Beeching was always proud that he had done the job asked of him and said, "I suppose I'll always be looked upon as the axe man, but it was surgery, not mad chopping."

Richard Russell was an 18th century doctor, who encouraged his patients to use the 'water cure', where they would bathe in, and drink, seawater. His medical practice began in Lewes, Sussex in 1725 and it was here that he published a *Dissertation on the Use of Sea Water in the Affections of the Glands*.

He recommended his patients try the seawater in Brighton and he built a house where the present day Royal Albion Hotel stands. His house was large enough to accommodate both his practice and many convalescing guests.

After Russell died in 1759 many royal visitors stayed at his house, including the Prince Regent in 1783. Over the next 40 years the prince would make his own court in Brighton and this was crucial in its development from a sleepy fishing village to a bustling town. A plaque on the wall of the Royal Albion Hotel reads: 'If you seek his monument, look around'.

On September 3rd 1658, **Richard Cromwell** succeeded his father, Oliver, and became 2nd Lord Protector of England, Scotland and Ireland. His reign would last for just eight months.

Richard had been passed over for membership of the Barebones Parliament by his father in 1653, despite his younger brother, Henry, being a member. Initially Oliver seemed concerned about his third son's ability to lead the country well.

In 1657, however, Cromwell decided to involve his son more deeply in politics. In July of that year he was made

Chancellor of Oxford University and, in December, he became a member of the council of state.

Cromwell also named him as his heir during this period.

When Richard became ruler he was mistrusted by both the military and the landed gentry, the two parts of society which controlled the country. His position was quickly compromised and he resigned his post on May 25th 1659.

The nursery rhyme, 'Hickory Dickory Dock', is reputed to refer to the brevity of Richard's reign.

An associate of the notorious Kray twins, **Richard Hart**, was murdered at Mr. Smith's Club in Catford on March 8th 1966. Ronnie Kray avenged Hart's death by shooting George Cornell in the Blind Beggar pub in Whitechapel Road.

According to sources, Ronnie Kray walked towards Cornell, took out a 9 mm Mauser and calmly shot him once in the forehead, just above his right eye. Cornell slumped against a nearby pillar, the bullet, apparently, passing straight through him.

Moments earlier the barmaid, who was later to become a key witness in the trial, had put a new record on the jukebox, The Sun Ain't Gonna Shine Anymore by The Walker Brothers. After the shooting the record stuck on the words 'anymore... anymore'.

Cornell's murder led to Kray's conviction and imprisonment for 32 years. He was released in 2000 but died of cancer a few weeks later.

Two Richards put their signatures to the United States Declaration of Independence:

Richard Stockton, a lawyer and legislator, was born near Princeton in New Jersey in 1730 and was elected to the Second Continental Congress in 1776.

Richard Henry Lee was from Virginia and is best known for proposing the motion in the Second Continental Congress calling for the colonies' independence from Great Britain.

He also argued that; "To preserve liberty, it is essential that the whole body of the people always possess arms, and be taught alike, especially when young, how to use them."

This has since become enshrined in the United States Constitution. He was the great uncle of Confederate general Robert E. Lee.

Of the 25 barons who were charged with enforcing the Magna Carta in 1215, three were named Richard.

Richard de Monfichet, who died in 1267, was an Essex landowner who provided surety that the document would be enacted properly.

Richard de Clare was a leading negotiator and also provided surety, as did **Richard de Percy**.

Magna Carta was the first document forced on to an English king by his subjects in an attempt to limit his powers by law. Although this did not really happen in practice in the Middle Ages, the version of Magna Carta issued in 1297 is still on the statute books of England and Wales.

It's most important and enduring legacy is the right of Habeus Corpus, which gives an individual the right of appeal against imprisonment.

The committee of 25 barons could meet at any time and overrule the will of the king through force by seizing his castles and possessions if necessary.

The 37th President of the United States was **Richard Milhous Nixon** (b. 1913).

His long career in politics began with his election to the House of Representatives in 1946. In 1950 he was elected to the Senate and in 1952 became vice president to Dwight Eisenhower for two terms.

Nixon contested the 1960 presidential election against John F. Kennedy and lost by 120,000 votes amidst claims of vote-rigging. Political commentators have speculated that his participation in the televised debate, and his decision not to shave beforehand, may have cost him the election.

In 1968 Nixon was successfully elected as US president by appealing to America's 'silent majority'. As president, Nixon co-ordinated the withdrawal of US troops from Vietnam. By 1973 he had reduced the American standing army from 543,000 to 0.

After becoming deeply embroiled in the 'Watergate' scandal Nixon became the only US president to resign on August 9th 1974.

He died in 1994, aged 81.

NOBEL PRIZE-WINNING RICHARDS

A number of Richards have won Nobel Prizes, including:

Richard Zsigmondy	Chemistry, 1925
Richard Kuhn	Chemistry, 1938
Richard Synge	Chemistry, 1952
Richard Stone	Economics, 1984
Richard Taylor	Physics, 1990
Richard Ernst	Chemistry, 1991
Richard Roberts	Medicine, 1993
Richard Smalley	Chemistry, 1996
Richard Axel	Medicine, 2004
Richard Schrock	Chemistry, 2005

Ig-Nobel Prize-winning Richards

The first Ig Nobels were awarded in 1991 for discoveries 'that cannot, or should not, be reproduced'.

1994 Medicine

Patient X, a victim of a venomous bite from his pet rattlesnake, for his determined use of electroshock therapy. At his own insistence, automobile spark plug wires were attached to his lip, and the car engine revved to 3,000 rpm for five minutes.

Dr. Richard C. Dart, of the Rocky Mountain Poison Center, and **Dr. Richard A. Gustafson** of The University of Arizona Health Sciences Center, for their well-grounded medical report, 'Failure of Electric Shock Treatment for Rattlesnake Envenomation'.

1997 Astronomy

Presented to **Richard C. Hoagland** for identifying artificial features including; a human face on Mars, and ten-mile high buildings on the far side of the moon.

1998 Economics

Presented to **Richard Seed** for his efforts to stimulate the world economy by cloning himself, and other human beings.

MURDEROUS RICHARDS

Richard Hickock (1931-1965) and his accomplice, Perry
Smith, murdered the Clutter family in Holcomb, Kansas
on the night of November 15th 1959. After hearing of the
Clutter family's vulnerability from an inmate he befriended
in Lansing prison, Hickock and Smith decided to invade the
family home and rob them of the money they reportedly
kept there.

The pair tied up the Clutter family and interrogated them
at gunpoint over the whereabouts of the house safe and
cash. After it had been revealed that there was no money
present, the two invaders moved the family to separate parts
of the house and then shot them, one by one.

The bodies were discovered the next morning by a friend
who was coming to meet them on the way to a church
service.

Hickock and Smith were captured in Las Vegas in a stolen
car. They were tried and found guilty of murdering the
Clutter family and executed by hanging.

The murder inspired Truman Capote's 'non-fiction novel'
In Cold Blood and Hickock has the dubious honour of being
played by three different actors in film adaptations of the
crime, and of Capote's life.

Also known as 'Lucky', **Richard Bingham** (1934-declared
legally dead in 1999), 7th Earl of Lucan is notorious as

Lord Lucan. He mysteriously vanished after the murder of the family nanny, Sandra Rivett, and both his location and status have been unknown since the night of November 8th 1974.

Bingham's wife alleges that he admitted to the killing of Rivett but claimed it had been a mistake. The coroner brought a verdict of unlawful killing and named Lucan as the murderer.

There have been many 'sightings' of Bingham around the world as far away as Australia, South Africa and India. It was claimed as recently as 2007 that Bingham was alive and living in New Zealand. So far, none of the investigations have proved to be the elusive peer.

Bingham's disappearance inspired the phrase 'doing a Lord Lucan' for someone who quickly and inexplicably goes missing.

Richard Lawrence has the reputation of being the first known person to attempt the assassination of a US president. He is described as a deranged Englishman who fantasised that he was, in fact, King Richard III.

In his delusion he maintained that he was owed a great deal of money by the American government but that President Andrew Jackson was preventing him from collecting his dues.

When the opportunity to shoot Jackson presented itself at the funeral of a congressman on January 30th 1835, both of Lawrence's pistols misfired and he was wrestled to the ground by the crowd.

At the trial Lawrence was found not guilty by reason of insanity and committed to spend the rest of his life in hospitals and institutions. He died in a Washington asylum in 1861.

Arrested on December 22nd 2001 for attempting to blow up American Airlines flight 63, **Richard Reid** has been dubbed the 'Shoe-bomber' by the media.

Reid had managed to board the plane, using an assumed name, after being refused permission the previous day.

Shortly after the mid-flight meal had been served Reid was observed trying to light a match. When challenged by the flight attendant Reid was found to be attempting to light a fuse on his shoe, which contained more than a hundred grams of plastic explosive in the sole – enough to blow a substantial hole in the aircraft.

After a struggle in the cabin, Reid was subdued with Valium and arrested after the flight was diverted to Boston airport.

Reid is currently serving life imprisonment in Florence, Colorado.

On May 8th 1979 **Richard Trenton Chase** (1950-1980) was found guilty of six counts of first degree murder and sentenced to die in the gas chamber.

'The Vampire of Sacramento' had been on a grisly killing spree, accounting for all of his victims in less than a month. Not only had Chase massacred the six, but he also engaged in acts of mutilation, vampirism and cannibalism and often took parts of his victims' bodies with him to chew on.

Chase ascribed his habit of drinking blood to the delusion that Nazis were trying to turn his blood into powder via a poison they had secreted underneath his soap dish.

He was found dead in his cell by a prison warden. Apparently he had committed suicide by taking an overdose of anti-depressants, encouraged by other prison inmates horrified by the violence of his crimes.

Over the course of one night in July 1966, **Richard Speck** (1941-1991) terrorised and murdered eight student nurses in their Chicago home. On the morning of July 16th a ninth visiting nurse, who had managed to hide under a bed, emerged from the house shouting, "They're all dead! All my friends are dead!"

Speck had broken into the house under the influence of alcohol and drugs, he claimed, and systematically separated the nurses from each other before stabbing or strangling them to death. Although he had confessed to the crime he later said he had no memory of the night.

Speck died of heart attack in prison one day before his fiftieth birthday.

His story has been made into two feature films and the news report of the crime plays in the background introduction to Simon and Garfunkel's version of *Silent Night.*

In just over a year, from June 1984 to August 1985, **Ricardo Ramirez** (b. 1960) claimed 14 victims in a terrible spree of violence, mutilation and murder.

Dubbed 'Nightstalker' by the press he terrorised the occupants of Los Angeles County.

The young Ramirez was impressed by the tales of killing and torture told to him by his cousin, Mike, an ex-Green Beret, who returned home from the Vietnam War when Ramirez was 12. According to his biographer, Ramirez and Mike spent a great deal of time together, smoking pot and talking about war victims.

When Mike's wife complained to him about his laziness he shot her in the face and killed her in front of Richard.

By the ninth grade, Ramirez was using drugs heavily and had dropped out of school. He was arrested on numerous occasions for possession of drugs and car theft. During this period he became interested in satanic rites and would often adorn his body with the Pentagram.

Ramirez had become an expert burglar and broke into the home of 79-year-old Jenny Vincow on the night of June 28th 1984 while she slept. He became angered that she had nothing of value to steal and he killed her by slashing her throat repeatedly. It was revealed at the post-mortem that she had been sexually assaulted. She was the first of his many victims.

On October 3rd 1996, Ramirez married Doreen Lioy in a prison service. The marriage has not been consummated and Lioy claims that she is still a virgin.

He is still on death row, pending appeals.

In 1924 **Richard Albert Loeb** (1905-1936), and his accomplice lover Nathan Leopold, sought to commit the perfect crime. A highly intelligent young man from a wealthy Chicago family, Loeb had graduated from the University of Michigan aged 17.

Obsessed by crime, Loeb read about, planned and committed a series of crimes increasing in severity – from petty theft to arson – and fantasised about carrying out a murder simply to do it. It was his idea to abduct and kill 14-year-old Bobby Franks, a relative.

They planned the murder for months and finally enticed Franks into their rented car on May 21st 1924. Once inside he was attacked with a chisel and had his throat stuffed. He died from a combination of blows to the head and suffocation. Loeb and Leopold then took the victim's body to Lake Wolf to dispose of it. They poured hydrochloric acid over the boy to make identification more difficult.

The pair then sent a ransom note to the boy's family demanding $10,000 be thrown from a train at a pre-arranged location. Unfortunately, for Loeb and Leopold, the boy's body was discovered before the ransom could be paid. Even more disastrous, Leopold's glasses were discovered near the body. They were made using a special hinge from a Chicago optician who had sold only three pairs of these spectacles.

Loeb and Leopold were arrested and pleaded guilty at the advice of their defence lawyer, Clarence Darrow. The skill of Darrow's anti-capital punishment plea meant that the two avoided the death penalty the media and public were clamouring for.

In January, 1936, Loeb was attacked in the prison shower by a fellow inmate with a razor. His assailant inflicted 58 wounds on his body, from which Loeb later died.

In 1931 **Reinhard Tristan Eugen Heydrich** was recruited to the Nazi counter-intelligence division of the SS by Heinrich Himmler. Nicknamed 'The Blonde Beast', he came to be admired by the Nazi high command for his systematic collection of information – real and falsified – about German citizens and politicians. The material he sought was usually the sordid, dirty secrets with which he could incriminate an individual.

In June 1934 Heydrich supplied Nazi leaders with a dossier of manufactured evidence, which allowed them to instigate the purge against their opposition. During 'The Night of the Long Knives' at least 85 people perished.

By 1936, Heydrich had been promoted by Himmler to head of the Gestapo and criminal police. Their partnership was key to the success of the party. Heydrich was looked upon favourably by Hitler, who often thought of him as a possible successor.

In September 1941, Heydrich was appointed Reichsprotektor of the Czech territories annexed by the Germans during the invasion of May 1939. Whilst in Prague, he worked tirelessly on the 'Final Solution', the Nazi plan to eradicate the Jews of Germany and Europe.

An attempt was made to assassinate Heydrich by the Czech government in exile. He was shot on May 27th, 1942 as his car drove through the Prague suburb of Kobylisy. He died from complications to his wounds eight days later.

The Nazis continued with their extermination of the Jews and the building of the first three death camps was called Operation Reinhard, in his honour.

Funny Richards

Although most famous as a stand-up comedian and star of hit television comedies, *The Office* and *Extras*, **Richard Dene 'Ricky' Gervais** (b. 1961) has also presented popular radio shows for XFM, Capital Radio and the BBC.

According to his website Gervais 'breezed a degree in Philosophy' at University College London (he was awarded a 2:2). He also formed the band Seona Dancing with fellow student Bill Macrae in 1983 and released two singles on Virgin records.

More to Lose charted at 70 in the UK but went on to have a life of it's own in the Philippines after it was picked up by a Manila DJ. The record became an anthem for angsty Filipino teenagers. Seona Dancing now has its own dedicated fansite with correspondents calling for the band to reform.

Gervais managed the band Suede before they were signed.

He is developing a career in film and has recently appeared in *Night at the Museum* (2006) and *Stardust* (2007) with Robert De Niro, for whom he was apparently mistaken by Swedish tourists in Los Angeles in July 2008.

After meeting Adrian Edmondson and Ben Elton at the University of Manchester in 1975, **Richard Michael 'Rik' Mayall** (b. 1958) embarked on a career in comedy that has lasted for almost thirty years. He and Edmondson debuted at The Comedy Store in London, appearing as 20th Century Coyote.

Mayall's first television role was that of 'roving reporter' Kevin Turvey, an investigative journalist from Redditch, on *A Kick up the Eighties* on BBC2 in 1981. Around the same time he and fellow comedians, who had formed their own company, began making *The Comic Strip Presents...* for Channel 4.

He also starred as Conservative MP Alan B'Stard in four series of *The New Statesman* on ITV from 1987-94, a role he reprised in a 2007 UK theatre tour.

After a serious quad bike accident in 1998, Mayall fractured his skull and fell into a coma for five days. After reviving he was convinced that the doctors were holding him hostage and tried to escape.

Mayall has a devoted female following at Hardbabe Central, a website founded in 2001, whose motto is, 'We love Rik's pants because he loves ours'.

Born on December 1st 1940 in his grandmother's brothel, black American funnyman **Richard Franklin Lennox Pryor III**, overcame an inauspicious start in life to become one of the most highly regarded comedians of all time. Fellow stand-up Jerry Seinfeld has called Pryor 'The Picasso of our profession'.

In 1963 Pryor moved to New York and began to work regularly as a stand-up comedian and opened for Nina Simone at New York nightclub Village Gate.

By 1969 Pryor was famous across America and appeared in sell-out shows in Las Vegas. He famously lost his nerve supporting Dean Martin and walked off stage after asking the packed audience, "What the fuck am I doing here". He became known, thereafter, for his heavy use of colourful language.

By the mid 1970s, Pryor was the guest host of NBC's *Saturday Night Live*, appearing with Dan Ackroyd, John Belushi and Chevy Chase. His own 1977 series, *The Richard Pryor Show*, was cancelled after only four episodes by nervous TV executives who thought Pryor's material was too controversial.

This didn't stop Pryor from releasing massively successful concert films *Live and Smokin'* (1971) and *Richard Pryor: Live on the Sunset Strip* (1982).

In 1983, he signed a five-year film contract with Columbia Pictures worth $40,000,000 and made *Superman III* (1983), *Brewster's Millions* (1985) and *Harlem Nights* (1989) with Eddie Murphy, who acknowledged Pryor's influence on his career.

In 2004 he was voted number one in Comedy Central's 100 Greatest Stand-ups list and passed away a year later.

Hailing from south London, black British comedian and television 'personality', **Richard Blackwood**, is the nephew of soul/funk singer Junior, who had a hit in the 1980s with Mama Used to Say.

Blackwood has presented his own TV variety show and appeared on numerous comedy sketch shows including *The Real McCoy* (1991-96).

He infamously took part in Chris Morris' *Brass Eye* special 'Paedogeddon' to talk about how internet paedophiles can make computer keyboards emit noxious fumes in order to subdue children.

When appearing on BBC2's *Never Mind the Buzzcocks*, Mark Lamar's introduction ran, "A man who can list on his CV rapper, comedian, presenter, actor, writer – all after the word 'failed' Superstar fantasist Richard Blackwood. Or as I think of him, 'Won't Smith'."

An ex-president of Cambridge University's Footlights amateur dramatics society, **Richard Ayoade** (b. 1977) has made critically acclaimed comedy series for Channel 4, including *Garth Merenghi's Darkplace* (2004) and spin-off talk show *Man to Man with Dean Lerner* (2006).

He was part of the original cast for *The Mighty Boosh* but had to pass on his role due to contractual obligations with Channel 4. He appeared in Chris Morris' *Nathan Barley* (2004) and plays Maurice Moss in *The IT Crowd*.

Ayoade also directs music videos and has made promos for Arctic Monkeys, Super Furry Animals and Vampire Weekend.

He directed Arctic Monkeys' concert film *At the Apollo* (2008). **Rich Hall** (b. 1954) is an American stand-up comedian, writer and TV presenter. He has appeared on UK TV panel comedy shows, such as *Have I Got News for You* and *Never Mind the Buzzcocks*. Hall is celebrated for his deadpan and somewhat grumpy delivery style.

Hall is an Emmy award-winning writer of *The Letterman Show* and won the Perrier Award for comedy at 2000's Edinburgh festival for his most famous comic creation Otis Lee Crenshaw, a character he has toured extensively.

He has written three comedy series for BBC television and in 2008 presented a documentary run for BBC4 about American Westerns, *How the West was Lost*.

Hall has published several books of 'sniglets', which are defined as 'any word that should appear in the dictionary but doesn't'. He invented the phrase and many such words, including 'sniffleridge', which is the groove running between the nose and the mouth.

A jobbing actor for much of the 1960s, **Richard O'Sullivan** (b. 1944) had small roles in television series like *Dixon of Dock Green* and *Father, Dear Father*. His breakthrough role was that of the brilliant and arrogant Dr. Lawrence Bingham in ITV's *Doctor…* comedies.

Admired for his comic timing, O'Sullivan was given the lead part of Robin Tripp in LWT's *Man About the House*, which ran for six series from 1973 to 1976 and spawned spin-off show *Robin's Nest*, which ran for 48 episodes from 1977 to 1981 and was the first UK sitcom to feature an unmarried couple cohabiting.

He also played highwayman **Dick Turpin** in ITV's series of the same name from 1979-82.

He appeared in two films with Cliff Richard; *The Young Ones* (1961) and *Wonderful Life* (1964).

O'Sullivan retired from acting in the late 1990s and suffered a stroke in 2003. He now resides in Brinsworth House, a retirement home for actors and entertainers and is fondly remembered by well-wishers on websites, such as boredatuni.com.

RADA trained actor, **Richard Wilson** (b. 1936) acted in repertory theatres for many years but is perhaps most well-known for his television comedy roles. He appeared with David Jason in four series of *A Sharp Intake of Breath* from 1977-81, and played the acerbic ward consultant, Gordon Thorpe, in *Only When I Laugh* (1979-82).

He is best known for playing Victor Meldrew in BBC's classic comedy *One Foot in the Grave*, which ran for six series and many specials from 1990 to 2000. The show was voted tenth best comedy in a BBC poll of Britain's Best Sitcoms in 2004.

Wilson was elected rector of Glasgow University for three years in 1996.

FOOD AND DRINK RICHARDS

In 2004 **Richard Corrigan** and Searcy's Ltd. opened
an exclusive restaurant and bar at the top of St Mary's
Axe, the striking Norman Foster-designed building known
affectionately as The Gherkin.

He has appeared on television many times, including stints
on *Masterchef, Saturday Kitchen* and Channel 4's *Jamie's Kitchen*.
He has also been a presenter on *Full on Food*. Richard was
a participant in the 2006 series of *Great British Menu* and
his smoked salmon starter went through to the final of the
competition.

Richard Fox is a chef, broadcaster and writer with 25
years of experience in the bar and catering industry. His
Food and Beer Cookbook was published in 2006. He established
the Beer and Food education programme for Leith's School
of Cookery, and regularly writes a Beer Chef column for
Maxim magazine.

Richard appeared in the BBC Two series *Food Poker* in
autumn 2007.

Rick Stein (b. 1947) is the first TV chef everyone thinks
of when it comes to seafood. His many TV programmes
and books include *Rick Stein's Taste of the Sea, Fruits of the Sea,
Seafood Odyssey, Fresh Food, Seafood Lovers' Guide, Food Heroes,
French Odyssey* and, most recently, *Mediterranean Escapes*.
In January 2003, he was awarded an OBE for services to

Cornish tourism. He is the uncle of Radio One DJ Judge Jules.

THE ROAD TO RICHARD

Richard Road, Rotherham
Richard Road, Seaforth, Liverpool
Richard Road, Darton, Barnsley
Richard Road, Walsall

Richard Street, Maerdy, Ferndale, Rhondda
Richard Street, Birmingham
Richard Street, Pontycymer, Bridgend

St Richard's Road, Dover, Kent
St Richard's Road, Otley, Leeds
St Richard's Road, Westergate, West Sussex

Richard's Castle is a village on the border between Herefordshire and Shropshire and lies between Leominster and Ludlow.

Richard Fitz Scrob (or Fitz Scrope) was a Norman knight granted lands by King Edward the Confessor before the Norman Conquest, in Herefordshire, Worcestershire and Shropshire as recorded in the Domesday Book.

He built Richard's Castle before 1051. It is thought to be the first castle built on English soil. The castle was a motte and bailey style construction, one of very few castles of this type built before the Norman Conquest.

CINEMATIC RICHARDS

Arch RADA 'luvvie' **Richard Attenborough** (b. 1923) is one of Britain's most successful and well-loved actors and directors. His mother was a founder of the Marriage Guidance Council and his father was a professor at Emmanuel College, Cambridge.

He started acting at 12 and studied at the Royal Academy of Dramatic Art until he enlisted for service in the RAF during World War II. He made his first film appearance in *In Which We Serve* (1942) and went on to appear in another 60 films, including *Brighton Rock* (1947) in which he played the role of psychopathic gangster, Pinkie, and *The Great Escape* (1963).

Despite his prolific acting career Attenborough has never been nominated for an Academy Award in an acting role. Attenborough made his directorial debut in 1969 with *Oh! What a Lovely War*. He also directed *A Bridge Too Far* (1977) and the box office sensation *Gandhi* (1982) which won many awards around the world, including that year's Oscar for Best Director.

He was awarded the CBE in 1967, was knighted in 1976 and was given a life peerage in 1993, so that his full title would be The Rt. Hon. The Lord Attenborough, CBE.

Attenborough is the President of RADA, Chairman of Capital Radio, President of BAFTA, President of the Gandhi Foundation, and President of the British National Film and Television School.

He has been married to Sheila Simm since 1945. The couple have lived in the same house in Richmond, Surrey since 1951.

Richard Tiffany Gere dropped out of the University of Massachusetts in 1969 after two years as a philosophy major to pursue a career in acting.

Established as a major actor by his role in *American Gigolo* (1980), Gere went on to star in the box office hit *An Officer and a Gentleman* (1982) as Zack Mayo, a navy recruit with a bad attitude, with Debra Winger.

His Hollywood career has been prolific and has produced other blockbuster films such as *Pretty Woman* (1990) and *Sommersby* (1993). Gere trained for five months for the tap-dancing scene in *Chicago* (2000).

A descendant of **Richard Warren**, a passenger on the *Mayflower*, Gere is well known as a humanitarian. He became interested in Buddhism on a trip to Nepal in 1978 after talking to many Tibetan exiles. He established the Gere Foundation in 1991 to assist those fighting for their human rights. He is a keen and active supporter of the Dalai Lama, for which he is banned permanently from the People's Republic of China.

Richard Ewing 'Dick' Powell began his show business career singing with the Charlie Davis Orchestra, with whom he made a number of records in the 1930s. After Warner

Brothers bought the company they recorded for, Powell was given a major film contract in 1932 and went on to play the lead 'crooner' in musicals such as *42nd Street* (1933).

Powell's career diversified in the 1950s as he directed a clutch of films, including *The Conqueror* (1956) starring John Wayne. The film is notorious for two reasons: it won the Golden Turkey award for the worst casting – John Wayne as Genghis Khan. But there is a darker reason for its infamy. The film was shot near St. George, Utah, a site which had been used for extensive nuclear testing.

By 1981, 91 of the 220 cast and crew had contracted cancer, 46 terminally, including Powell.

Better known as **Richard Burton** (1925-1984), Richard Walter Jenkins was the twelfth of thirteen children. Born in the Welsh mining village of Pontrhydyfen, Burton was a keen scholar and sportsman, excelling at rugby and cricket.

His interest in English and Welsh literature brought him to the attention of his mentor, Philip Burton, from whom he adopted his surname. The two became extremely close, with the elder Burton tutoring the younger intensely in literature and theatre.

Burton won a special scholarship to Exeter College, Oxford, to study acting for six months in 1943. After his discharge from the RAF in 1947, Burton made his way to London to pursue a career in acting. He starred in his first film, *The Last Days of Dolwyn* in 1949.

In 1963 Burton appeared opposite Elizabeth Taylor in Cleopatra. It was the film that would ignite their passionate on-off romance. They were married and divorced twice. Burton said of their partnership: "Our love is so furious we burn each other out." The pair co-starred in eleven films.

Renowned for his deep and resonant voice, Burton voiced many radio plays, including *Under Milk Wood* (1954). He was the narrator for Jeff Wayne's *War of the Worlds* (1978) and has recorded anthologies of the poems of Dylan Thomas.

Born into a working class New York family, **Richard Bright** was the youngest of four brothers named after English kings.

He is probably most famous for the role of Al Neri, Michael Corleone's personal bodyguard, in Francis Ford Copolla's Godfather trilogy. He played the cold-eyed assassin in all three films.

His other notable films include *The Getaway* (1972) with Steve McQueen and Ali McGraw, *Marathon Man* (1976) and *Once Upon a Time in America* (1984) with Robert De Niro and James Woods.

Bright was also a keen stage actor and was noted for his portrayal of Richard III.

The 7ft 2ins. **Richard Kiel** (b. 1939) has made a successful film career playing tall lumbering henchmen. His most widely seen role is that of Jaws in two James Bond films; *The Spy Who Loved Me* (1977) and *Moonraker* (1979).

During filming, Kiel could only wear the steel teeth for a few moments at a time as they cut into his gums and made him gag by pushing his tongue back. There was an intense internet debate about whether the cables he bites into on film are made of liquorice.

He was originally chosen to play the Hulk in the 1970s TV adaptation but was later replaced by Lou Ferrigno.

Kiel published his autobiography *Making it BIG in the Movies* in 2002.

As a conscientious objector during the Vietnam War, **Richard Dreyfuss** (b. 1947) picked up small roles in television and film while living in his adopted home of Los Angeles.

His first film of note was *Dillinger* (1973) and he appeared again that year in *American Graffiti* with Harrison Ford. Momentum was building for Dreyfuss' film career and he starred in two of the biggest movies of the 1970s; *Jaws* (1975) and *Close Encounters of the Third Kind* (1976), both directed by Steven Spielberg. He won the Oscar for best actor for *The Goodbye Girl* (1977). Aged 30 he was, at the time, the youngest actor to win the award.

After a highly publicised battle with drugs in the 1980s, Dreyfuss revived his Hollywood career with *Down and Out in Beverly Hills* (1986), which also starred Nick Nolte and Bette Midler.

He is set to play **Dick Cheney** in Oliver Stone's forthcoming biopic of George W. Bush, *W.*

Best known as 'the black private dick that's the sex machine to all the chicks', **Richard Roundtree** (b. 1942) starred in three films as John Shaft. *Shaft* (1971) was followed by *Shaft's Big Score* (1972) and *Shaft in Africa* (1973). His salary for *Shaft* was reported to be $12,500.

He won a football scholarship to Southern Illinois University and was chosen to be a part of the Ebony fashion tour. Roundtree decided to try a career in acting and became a member of New York's Negro Ensemble Company in 1967. Other famous alumni of the acting group include Denzel Washington and Samuel L. Jackson.

In 1993, Roundtree was diagnosed with a very rare form of male breast cancer and is now an advocate talking about the importance of early detection.

He provided the voice for the PlayStation character Akuji the Heartless.

Better known as 'Treat', **Richard Williams** is a stage and screen actor who has appeared in more than 75 films. He first appeared on film in *Deadly Hero* (1976) but it was his role in Milos Foreman's adaptation of *Hair* (1979) that led him to stardom.

Other notable Williams films include *1941* (1979), *Things to do in Denver When You're Dead* (1995) and *Once Upon a Time in America* (1984) in which he plays a union boss indebted to Robert De Niro's band of thugs. In one scene he is threatened by Chicken Joe pouring petrol over him, a character played by Richard Bright.

Williams's nickname comes from an ancestor on his mother's side, Robert Treat Paine, who is a signatory on the Declaration of Independence.

A stocky Italian-American television and film actor, **Richard Castellano**'s (1933-1988) most celebrated role is that of 'Fat' Pete Clemenza, a captain in the mafia family of *The Godfather* (1972).

As Clemenza, he taught the young Michael Corleone how to make spaghetti sauce for twenty men and instructed him how to shoot a small pistol in order to kill the family's most deadly adversaries.

He also utters the immortal line "It's a Sicilian message – it means Luca Brasi sleeps with the fishes," after the Corleone family assassin's bullet-proof vest has been delivered to the house wrapped with dead fish.

Castellano was often typecast as burly criminals and directors generally insisted that this already overweight man gain fifty pounds for his screen roles. He was nominated for Best Supporting Actor at the academy awards for *Lovers and Other Strangers* (1970).

The multi-talented **Richard St. John Harris** (1930-2002), a renowned stage and screen actor, is also highly regarded as a film director, a singer-songwriter, a theatrical producer and poet.

The fifth of eight children, whose parents owned a flour mill, Harris was a talented sportsman as a youth, excelling at rugby. His sporting activity was ended after a bout of tuberculosis as a teenager.

His breakthrough film was *This Sporting Life* (1963) for which he received an Oscar nomination for Best Actor. On hearing this he declared "I've struck a blow for the Irish rebellion."

A lifelong fan of rugby, Harris would often watch matches with his friends Peter O'Toole and Richard Burton, of whom there are stories of drunken antics. Harris himself disappeared on a drinking binge for three weeks after chancing upon the news that Young Munster were playing. He took the next flight from London to Ireland and on his return asked his wife "Why didn't you pay the ransom?" before she could ask where he had been.

His notable films include *Camelot* and *A Man Called Horse* (both 1970) and he appeared as Albus Dumbledore in two Harry Potter films.

In 1968, Harris had an American number two hit with MacArthur Park.

Inspired to a comedy career by Stan Laurel, with whom he became great friends, the TV and film actor and presenter, better known as **Dick Van Dyke** (b.1925) has been a show business personality for more than five decades.

He has starred in two long-running TV comedy shows *The Dick Van Dyke Show* (1961-66) and *The New Dick Van Dyke Show* (1971-74) and was the lead in the medical crime drama *Diagnosis: Murder* (1992-2001).

In 1964 Van Dyke played the chirpy Cockney chimney sweep, Bert, in *Mary Poppins*. The English accent he tried for this is notorious as one of the worst attempts on film. He did, however, win an Oscar for best song for Chim Chim Cher-ee, co-written by **Richard M. Sherman**. His other film of note is *Chitty Chitty Bang Bang* (1968).

Van Dyke sings bass in a barbershop quartet called The Vantastix. He was made a lifelong member of The Society for the Preservation and Encouragement of Barbershop Quartet Singing in America (SPEBSQSA) in 1999.

The American actor, **Richard Crenna**, appeared in more than 70 films and is best known for his portrayal of Colonel Samuel Trautman in the first three Rambo films.

His career began in the radio series *Our Miss Brooks* (1948-57) as the character Walter Denton. He later played Luke McCoy on television in *The Real McCoys* (1957-62). His notable films include *Jonathan Livingstone Seagull* (1973), *Body Heat* (1981) and *The Flamingo Kid* (1984).

His star is two down from Sylvester Stallone's on the Hollywood Walk of Fame.

Nominated for an Academy Award for Best Supporting Actor for his first film *Kiss of Death* in 1947, **Richard Widmark** (1914-2008) notched up appearances in more than 60 films. He established himself as a dynamic 'film noir' actor during the 1940s and 1950s with films like *Night and the City* (1950) but also adapted to roles in many westerns.

He played Jim Bowie in *The Alamo* (1960) directed by and starring John Wayne and appeared in the classic *How the West Was Won* in 1962.

Widmark demonstrated further versatility by acting as a Norseman in *The Long Ships* (1964) and playing the eponymous New York police detective *Madigan* (1968).

Green City, Missouri named its airport after him after a donation of funds.

A stage actor from the age of seven, **Richard Earl Thomas** (b. 1951) made his television debut in a production of Ibsen's *A Doll's House* in 1959, with Julie Harris and Christopher Plummer.

Although he has acted widely and for more than 40 years, Thomas will be forever familiar as the bespectacled John-Boy Walton, the aspiring writer from the hit TV series *The Waltons* (1972-81). Thomas played the role for 122 episodes and made numerous guest appearances until a 'new' John-Boy was cast.

On stage, Thomas has played Richard II and has a supporting role in *Wonder Boys* (2000) starring Michael Douglas.

A familiar face to many cinemagoers, American character actor **Richard Jenkins** has had roles in more than 50 films, including *Hannah and Her Sisters* (1986), *There's Something about Mary* (1998) and *The Man Who Wasn't There* (2001). His first starring role is as economics professor Walter Vale, in 2008's *The Visitor.*

His most famous role is that of Nathaniel Fisher, the head of a family funeral home in HBO's *Six Feet Under*. The character is killed in the pilot episode of the drama and subsequently appears as a ghost to the other members of the cast for five seasons.

A young prodigy, **Richard Lester** studied clinical psychology at the University of Pennsylvania at the age of 15 and graduated at 19. He then worked in various roles in television, his aim to be a director.

He moved to London in 1953 and began directing low-budget TV variety shows. His work was noticed by Peter Sellers and he helped Sellers and the other stars of *The Goon Show* translate their work to the small screen.

In 1960 he made *The Running, Jumping and Standing Still Film* with Sellers and fellow Goon, Spike Milligan. It was shot over two weekends and cost £70. The film was a favourite of The Beatles and they chose Lester to direct *A Hard Day's Night* (1964) and *Help!* (1965). The energetic quick-cut style of these two films has been said to have influenced the music video. Lester was given an honorary 'Father of the Music Video Award' by MTV.

When he learned about this dubious tribute, he asked for a blood test.

Ruben Sax became a successful Hollywood screenwriter, producer and director using the alias **Richard Brooks**. His first screenplay was *Key Largo* (1948) starring Humphrey Bogart and Lauren Bacall.

He received six Oscar nominations, including *Cat on a Hot Tin Roof* (1958) and finally won the award for *Elmer Gantry* in 1960.

Brooks adapted Truman Capote's true crime novel *In Cold Blood* for the cinema and chose two unknowns to play the lead parts after he was turned down by Steve McQueen and Paul Newman. He was such a stickler for detail that he insisted on filming in the family home where the Clutters had been murdered and using real family photographs in the background.

He was married to Hollywood actresses Jean Brooks (1941-44) and Jean Simmons (1965-77).

The Texan **Richard Linklater** (b. 1960) cut short his university education and went to work on an oil rig in the Gulf of Mexico. He used money he earned on the rig to buy himself a Super8 camera and began to experiment with film-making.

In 1985 he founded the Austin Film Society to support and promote independent film. To date the society has made grants of over $500,000.

Linklater made *Slacker* (1991) for $23,000 and still has a commitment to making low budget pictures.

His films commonly take place in one day and are celebrated for the intimacy and compassion with which the characters are portrayed.

Notable films include *Dazed and Confused* (1993), *Waking Life* (2001) and *A Scanner Darkly* (2006) an adaptation of Philip K. Dick's novel.

Musical Richards

Better known as Ringo Starr, **Richard Starkey** was the last member to join The Beatles, replacing drummer Pete Best in 1962.

He was the first member to leave the Fab Four. During the recording of The White Album (1968) Ringo became dissatisfied with the constant band in-fighting and took two weeks' holiday with Peter Sellers. When he returned to the recording sessions he found his drums covered with flowers by the other Beatles.

Starr has also provided vocals for Beatles songs, including 'With A Little Help From My Friends' and 'What Goes On'. He has sole song-writing credits for 'Don't Pass Me By' and 'Octopus's Garden'.

Starr has had a prolific solo recording career and his most successful and acclaimed album was Ringo, produced by **Richard Perry**. It features musical contributions from the other ex-Beatles, something he was keen to encourage.

Kentucky 'old-time' folk musician, **Dick Burnett,** is noted for his great influence on American folk music. As a young adult Burnett was shot in the face during a robbery and was blinded in both eyes. As a result, he had to give up his job working in oil fields, but his boss proclaimed that he would make it as a musician.

He made his first recordings in 1926 and toured extensively in the Deep South with Leonard Rutherford, his musical partner for many years.

Burnett is credited with writing the folk classic 'A Man of Constant Sorrow', which is featured in the Coen brothers' film *O Brother, Where Art Thou?* (2000).

He died in January 1977, aged 94.

American teen-idol **Rick(y) Nelson** started his recording career in 1957 with a cover of Fats Domino's, I'm Walkin'. He only made the record because a girl he wanted to date told him that she was a crazy Elvis Presley fan. The song reached number four on the American charts.

He is often acknowledged as the first young star to use television as a medium to sell records. And because of this he is second only to Elvis as the most popular rock and roll artist of the 1950s and 60s.

His song Poor Little Fool became the first number one on Billboard's Hot 100 in August 1958.

Nelson was killed in a plane crash on New Year's Eve, 1985, while on a revival tour.

Paul Richard 'Rick' Buckler was the powerhouse drummer for The Jam, a highly successful mod-revival band, who were at their height from 1977 to 1982. With

The Jam, Buckler enjoyed 18 consecutive Top 40 hits and four number ones, including Town Called Malice and Going Underground.

Since The Jam spilt, Buckler has played in The Gift (2005) and re-united with Jam bassist, Bruce Foxton to tour as From The Jam (both playing their highly popular back catalogue) from 2006 onwards.

Singer-songwriter and guitarist **Richard Hawley** has released five critically acclaimed albums, including Coles' Corner in 2005, which was nominated for the following year's Mercury music prize. On discovering that his band, The Arctic Monkeys, had won, lead singer Alex Turner declared, "Someone call 999, Richard Hawley's been robbed".

His fondness for his hometown of Sheffield is reflected in his habit of naming albums and songs after the city's landmarks, including Lady's Bridge and Lowedges.

Hawley is a keen supporter of Sheffield Wednesday and proud of his working-class roots.

Richard Myers is better known as punk-singer **Richard Hell**. He formed the Neon Boys with Tom Verlaine in 1969 and they set about writing music together.

Their 1973 demo, which includes Love Comes in Spurts, is often touted as being the first punk recording. In 1974, Hell and Verlaine were joined by another guitarist and changed their name to Television. The band went on to become one of New York's most influential early punk groups and are credited with starting the scene which gravitated around the club CBGBs.

They built the stage that would also host The Ramones, Blondie and Talking Heads.

By 1976, Hell had left Television and formed Richard Hell and the Voidoids. They were famous for their first album Blank Generation and the title song was voted one of punk's all time Top Ten in *The Rough Guide to Punk* (2006).

Vegan and 'Simpleton' techno musician, **Richard Melville Hall** (b. 1965), is better known to the world as Moby. According to Moby the name was earned by being a distant relative of American author Herman Melville, who wrote *Moby Dick*.

The release of his second single, Go, in 1992 catapulted him to international attention. The record reached number ten in the UK charts.

Moby's sixth album, Play, released in 1999 became famous as the first record to have all of its tracks licensed for use in films, television and advertising, a ploy which drew criticism from many in the music industry. The album, which sampled heavily from the collected work of American folklorist, Alan Lomax, has sold more than ten million copies.

Moby is a committed Christian and animal welfare activist.

Richard Charles Rodgers is one of America's leading composers of songs for stage, musicals and film, with over 900 published songs and 40 musicals to his credit. His partnership with Oscar Hammerstein II is the most successful in musical theatre. The pair wrote musicals *Oklahoma!* (1943), *South Pacific* (1949) for which they won a Pulitzer prize, *The King and I* (1951) and *The Sound of Music* (1959).

Many of their creations were adapted successfully for the cinema and their songs still endure in popular culture. *The Sound of Music* won five Oscars as well as saving 20th Century Fox from bankruptcy after the excesses of filming *Cleopatra* (1963). The music to the film has never been out of print.

The soundtrack album for *The Sound of Music* was included in the stockpile of records held in 20 underground radio stations of Great Britain's Wartime Broadcasting Service, designed to provide public information and morale-boosting broadcasts for 100 days after a nuclear attack.

Rodgers' song You'll Never Walk Alone, from *Carousel* (1945), has become a popular football terrace song and has been adopted as the anthem of Liverpool Football Club.

Rick Wakeman began his musical career as a session musician and played piano on David Bowie's Life on Mars, and the Cat Stevens hit Morning has Broken.

At the height of his session career, Rick was doing 18 a week. It is estimated that he has performed on over 2,000 different tracks by artistes as diverse as Black Sabbath, Mary Hopkins, Cilla Black, Clive Dunn, Elton John, Lou Reed, Dana, Des O'Connor, Al Stewart, Ralph McTell, and Harry Nilsson.

He is most famous as the spangley-caped multi-keyboardist with 1970s prog-rock group Yes. Wakeman joined the band in 1971 and appeared on their album of that year Fragile. He left Yes in May, 1974 after feeling he had nothing more to contribute.

Wakeman's solo career was launched by his album The Six Wives of Henry VIII (1973), followed by the Myths and Legends of King Arthur and the Knights of the Round Table LP in 1975. The latter was taken on a tour which involved an orchestra, a choir and a show on ice. Although the tour sold out the costs caused Wakeman to declare bankruptcy.

Richard Fairbrass (b. 1953) is the lead singer with musical duo, Right Said Fred. Their first single, Too Sexy, stayed at number two in the UK charts for six weeks. It might have made the number one spot but for Bryan Adams' blockbuster, Everything I Do (I Do it For You).

All of their first three singles made the UK top three and Deeply Dippy gave the band their only number one.

Right Said Fred enjoyed huge popularity in Germany and South Africa and their single, You're My Mate, stayed in the German Top 100 for 23 weeks. It was also adopted by the Springboks rugby team as their official anthem in 2002.

The band has recorded seven albums, the second of which, Up, reached number one in the UK in 1992.

Along with fellow techno DJs Jeff Mills and Carl Craig, **Richie Hawtin** is part of the 'second wave' of DJs from the influential city of Detroit. He has recorded and toured under various aliases, including Plastikman, F.U.S.E and Concept 1. He is a pioneer of 'minimal' techno.

Richard Archer (b. 1973) is the singer, guitarist and songwriter for Staines band, Hard-Fi. His lyrics reflect the frustration of living in a town where 'There's no record shops, there's no decent pubs, there's no venues, there's no decent clothes shops'.

Hard-Fi's debut album, Stars of CCTV (2003) was recorded in a local disused mini-cab office, reputedly for £300. After release on independent label, Necessary Records, the album was picked up by Atlantic Records and went on to become a number one.

The follow-up, 2007's Once Upon a Time in the West, also hit the number one spot.

After making it into the final ten of the first *Pop Idol* in 2002, **Rik Waller** had to withdraw from the show because he had severe laryngitis. After the show's run he signed a record deal with EMI reported to be worth £200,000. His first single was a cover version of Dolly Parton's song 'I Will Always Love You', which reached number 6 in the UK charts.

To help with his constant battle against being overweight, Waller appeared on ITV's *Celebrity Fit Club* in 2002. He was the first to leave the show.

A founder member of Sheffield's seminal Cabaret Voltaire, **Richard H. Kirk** has been on the cutting edge of experimental electronic music making for over 35 years. Formed in 1973, they had their first release on Rough Trade with 1978's Extended Play EP, the first release by the label.

The band also appeared on the Fac2 sampler released by Manchester's Factory Records in the same year. His solo release schedule has earned him the reputation of 'contemporary techno's busiest man'.

Richard Cole (b. 1946) was tour manager for rock and roll giants Led Zeppelin from 1968 to 1970 after having had a stint organising road trips for The Who.

In May 1973 suspicion fell on Cole when more than $180,000 of the band's money disappeared from their New York hotel. Cole had the key to the safe deposit box. He was the first to discover the loss of the money but neither he nor anyone from the band was charged with the theft. The money was never recovered and Led Zeppelin later sued the hotel.

After being sacked from the band Cole was mistakenly imprisoned after a terrorist attack in Italy. While in prison he managed to overcome his heroin addiction. On release he was so broke he had to work as a scaffolder.

Cole has also tour-managed Eric Clapton, Ozzy Osbourne and Black Sabbath.

His 1992 book *Stairway to Heaven: Led Zeppelin Uncensored*, was slammed by the band as 'permanently distorted'. Jimmy Page even considered suing Cole. Despite this he was invited to the VIP area for the band's 2007 reunion concert.

Dubbed 'The Prince of Romance' by Nancy Sinatra, French pianist Phillippe Pages is better known to the world as **Richard Clayderman** (b. 1953). He is famous for his orchestral piano arrangements of popular songs, which often end up as background muzak. Clayderman is happy to be associated with elevator music as he feels that he helps to brighten up busy lives.

Staggeringly successful, Clayderman has sold more than 70 million records (more than Robbie Williams and Shania Twain) and has been awarded 267 gold, and 70 platinum, discs.

Richard Berry (1935-1997) is celebrated as the original writer and performer of Louie Louie. Written in 1955 for a recording with The Pharoahs, Berry intended the song to be used as a B-side.

Louie Louie was recorded by The Kingsmen in 1963 and has become recognised as one of the most important versions of the song. Over 1,000 versions have been performed and recorded by artists as diverse as The Who, The Beach Boys, The Troggs, Motorhead and The Clash.

In 1983 KFJC, a college radio station in Los Altos Hills, California, played it for 63 hours straight without repeating the same recording twice! The event was dubbed Maximum Louie Louie and was attended by the writer of the song.

It was filmed with the intention of making a documentary but this has yet to appear. The song even has its own dedicated fansite www.louielouie.net.

Berry's song was the subject of an investigation by the FBI in February 1964 after a complaint by a disturbed American parent about the apparently obscene lyrics. However, as the FBI could not interpret the lyrics correctly no conclusion could be reached.

Along with Neil Young, Stephen Stills and Jim Messina, **Richie Furay** was a founding member of the influential folk-rock band Buffalo Springfield. The band, which took its name from the side of a tractor, is probably best known for the song, For What It's Worth, released in January, 1967.

Although later adopted by the anti-Vietnam War protestors the song was actually written to highlight Stephen Stills' concern at the confrontation between police and regulars at the closing of West Hollywood club, Pandora's Box.

Brooklyn-born singer and guitarist **Richie Havens** emerged from the same 1960s Greenwich Village music scene which nurtured Joan Baez and Bob Dylan.

He was the opening performer at the 1969 Woodstock Festival. Although initially billed fifth, Havens took the stage first as the road back to the artists' hotel was blocked. He ended up playing for nearly three hours, running out of songs but being called back by the crowd for encore after encore.

With nothing left to play he improvised a version of Motherless Child, adding the word freedom sung over and over. His version of the song was featured in the Woodstock film and became an international hit.

His performance at the festival established Havens' reputation as a performer and he played at the Isle of Wight festival in 1969 and at 1970's first ever Glastonbury festival.

Havens has continued to be a busy performer and recording artist. In 2000 he recorded two songs (Hands of Time and Little by Little) with British electronic duo, Groove Armada.

Dick Haymes (1918-1980) was one of the most popular balladeers of the 1940s and 1950s. In the mid 1930s he was hired by MGM studios as a stuntman and extra but slowly worked his way up to lead actor, appearing in films with stars such as Betty Grable and Ava Gardner.

He is most noted for his round baritone and is often hailed as one of the best singers of the twentieth century. He had long stints with the Harry James, Benny Goodman and Tommy Dorsey orchestras.

Haymes was born in Buenos Aires but lived most of his life in the United States. He never became a fully-fledged US citizen and used his legal alien status to avoid the World War II draft in 1944. He was nearly deported for his stand against the conflict and was imprisoned for a short time at Ellis Island in New York.

He wed six times, including a two-year marriage to Rita Hayworth.

Nicknamed 'The Beak' by his friends because of his sharply prominent nose, **Richard Manuel** was a talented multi-instrumentalist (comfortable on sax, harmonica and drums; and a virtuoso pianist and singer) with The Band.

Formed in 1967 from the members of Ronnie Hawkins' band, The Hawks, The Band had accompanied Bob Dylan on his 1965-66 world tour. Around the globe they endured the taunts and boos of loyal folk fans irate at Dylan's development of a more electric sound.

Manuel was noted for his energy and searing falsetto voice. Fellow band member **Rick Danko** said of him: "It was like having a force of nature in the band." His passionate performances were a highlight of The Band's live shows.

Unfortunately, Manuel was troubled by alcohol and drug problems throughout his career. By 1974, according to band-mate Levon Helm, Manuel was consuming around eight bottles of Grand Marnier a day.

All this was on top of an already huge cocaine addiction.

By the time The Band split in 1976 Manuel was firm friends with Eric Clapton and was the driving force behind his album of that year, No Reason To Cry. During that same year director Martin Scorcese had made a documentary of The Band's final concert. He was later invited by Scorcese to contribute to the soundtrack for *Raging Bull* (1980).

The Band reconvened in 1983 but Manuel's addictions and downward spiral continued. The death of The Band's manager, Albert Grossman in 1983, depressed him greatly and his mood continued to blacken.

After a gig on March 4th 1986, Manuel was found hanging in his hotel room. He was 42.

American saxophonist **Dick Stabile** (1909-1980) is reputed to be the only man who could play the highest note on the sax, 'a full octave above the top range of a saxophone'.

The head of Columbia Records, producer **Rick Rubin**, has been described by MTV as 'the most important producer of the last 20 years'.

He co-founded DefJam records with Russell Simmons whilst still a student at New York University in 1984. Among the label's early releases were the Rubin-produced albums Licensed to Ill (1986) and Raising Hell (1986), which were debuts for the Beastie Boys and Run-DMC, respectively.

He is credited with combining rock and hip hop, which found its best examples in Run-DMC's Walk This Way, and the Beastie Boys' Fight For Your Right (To Party). The two songs were massive hits on both sides of the Atlantic.

Rubin has also produced records for rock bands, including The Cult and Red Hot Chili Peppers. He was at the helm for the breakthrough Chili Peppers album Blood Sugar Sex Magik (1991).

In 1993 he held a full New Orleans-style funeral for the word Def after he heard that it had become an entry in the American dictionary.

From 1994 Rubin was producer of Johnny Cash's *American* series of albums.

He has won seven Grammy Awards.

Hired by Motown supremo Berry Gordy in 1961, **Richard 'Pistol' Allen** was a drummer for the label's house band The Funk Brothers. He played on many Motown hits including Heatwave, by Martha and the Vandellas, Reach Out I'll Be There, by the Four Tops and Heard It Through The Grapevine, by Marvin Gaye.

The story of The Funk Brothers has not been widely known until the recent documentary, *Standing in the Shadows of Motown* (2002) described the band's role.

The film claims that The Funk Brothers have 'played on more number one hits than The Beatles, Elvis, The Rolling Stones and The Beach Boys combined'.

After a battle with cancer, Allen died in June 2002, aged 69, in Detroit.

Singer **Richard Ashcroft** first formed The Verve in 1989. Their debut album A Storm in Heaven was released four years later.

Urban Hymns was released to great acclaim in 1997 and has sold more than 8 million copies. By 1999, however, it was all over for The Verve and they split amid much acrimony.

Ashcroft released the first of his three solo albums in 2000. Alone With Everybody went to number one in the

UK and gave him two top twenty singles. The other two albums, Human Condition (2002) – which featured a guest appearance by Beach Boy Brian Wilson – and Keys to the World (2006), were also top three sellers in the UK. The latter was only kept off the number one spot by the phenomenal sales of Arctic Monkeys' debut.

In July, 2006 Ashcroft was arrested for forcing entry into a youth club in Chippenham, Wiltshire, claiming he wanted to work with the youngsters. He was held by the police and fined £80 for disorderly behaviour after he refused to leave.

Famously derisive of modern culture Ashcroft declared in a 2005 interview, "We're in a malaise. What do people really believe in any more apart from sport and music?"

Better known as Aphex Twin, **Richard David James** has been described as 'the most inventive and influential figure in contemporary electronic music'.

His first release was the Analogue Bubblebath EP in 1991. That same year he also started his label Rephlex Records and coined the term 'braindance' to explain his uncategorisable music.

James's music is extremely sonically diverse and ranges from the delicate synthesizer ambience of 1992's Selected Ambient Works 85-92 to the treated and retuned pianos of 2001's Drukqs.

Born in Leipzig, Germany in May 1813, **Richard Wagner** has been called the greatest composer of the Romantic period. He is celebrated for his operas, particularly the Ring Cycle, *Der Ring des Niebelungen* (first performed between 1869 and 1874).

The later period of Wagner's work (1865-1882) is considered to be the zenith of the Romantic opera. *Tristan und Isolde* (1865) is widely acknowledged as one of the peaks of the operatic repertoire. The opera's opening chord (F,B,D#,G#) has become known as 'The Tristan Chord' and became a major influence on 20th century composers such as Claude Debussy and Arnold Schoenberg.

The Ring Cycle consists of four operas based on Teutonic myths and legends. The cycle took Wagner 26 years to complete and takes around 15 hours to perform in its entirety.

Richard Paul 'Rick' Astley began his musical career as the tea boy at Stock, Aitken and Waterman's Hit Factory studio.

His first single was 1987's Never Gonna Give You Up – the biggest selling UK single of the year – which spent five weeks at the top of the UK charts.

Astley remained quiet for most of the late 1990s and early 2000s but emerged from his self imposed obscurity with his 2002 release Keep it Turned On.

In August 2008 he was a headline act at the Northampton Balloon Festival.

British record producer **Richard X** (real name Philips) is well known for his bootleg, 'mash-up' style of amalgamating old electronic pop songs with those of new artists.

The most notable example of this is 2002's number one single, Freak Like Me, by Sugababes which featured extended samples of Tubeway Army's 1979 hit Are Friends Electric.

OUTER-SPACE RICHARDS

Richard A. Searfoss was selected for astronaut duties by NASA in 1991. On space shuttle *Columbia* in 1993 he completed 225 orbits, performing medical experiments on himself and lab animals. He flew again on the shuttle *Atlantis* in 1996 and spent 16 days on *Spacelab* in April 1998.

In 1996, **Richard M. Linnehan** went into space aboard *Columbia*. The shuttle journeyed more than 7 million miles in 405 hours and 48 minutes. Linnehan has orbited the earth 942 times over four missions.

An ex-operational fighter pilot, **Richard O. Covey** flew 339 combat missions for the USAF during two tours of duty in South-East Asia. He has made four space flights and logged over 640 hours outside the earth's atmosphere.

He was the first astronaut to pilot a space shuttle after the *Challenger* disaster of January 28th 1986, which claimed the life of fellow astronaut **Francis Richard 'Dick' Scovey**.

Richard F. Gordon Jr. (b.1929) was first launched into space on Gemini 11, alongside his long-time friend Pete Conrad. He is also part of the elite band of 24 men who has flown to the moon. A crew member of Apollo 12, with Conrad again and Alan Bean, Gordon was designated the command module pilot and had to orbit the moon while his fellows walked on the lunar surface.

Gordon was scheduled to walk on the moon as commander of Apollo 18, but the mission was cancelled due to budgetary restrictions.

On November 19th 2005, he was honoured as an Ambassador of Exploration by NASA.

Pilot **Richard N. Richards** flew into space on August 1981 aboard space shuttle *Columbia* on her maiden voyage. He has clocked up 33 days and 21 hours in space.

Richard Robert 'Ricky' Arnold is due to fly on NASA flight STS119, due for launch in winter 2008.

THE RICHEST RICHARDS

(Source: *Sunday Times Rich List 2008*)

The richest British Richard is entrepreneur **Sir Richard Branson** (b. 1950), who is worth £2,700 million. He left school at 16 and moved to London where he started *Student* magazine, his first successful business.

While travelling in France he bought cheap records which he then sold at markets from the boot of his car. By 1970 he had graduated to a mail order record business. His first Virgin record store opened in Notting Hill Gate in 1971.

In 1972 Branson helped to establish Virgin Records. The label's first release was Mike Oldfield's *Tubular Bells* (1973). Virgin became known for its prog-rock and Krautrock output until 1977, when the label signed punk band The Sex Pistols.

The head office shop was raided by the police after the band's album Never Mind the Bollocks, Here's the Sex Pistols appeared in the window. Virgin also introduced Culture Club to the world.

Branson sold Virgin Records to EMI in 1992 for $1 billion in order to prop up his Virgin Atlantic airline, which he founded in 1982.

Amongst his other business ventures are Virgin Trains (est. 1997), Virgin Mobile (1999), Virgin Galactic (2004) and Virgin Health Bank (2007), which offered parents-to-be the opportunity to store their baby's umbilical cord blood stem cells in private and public stem cell banks.

Branson is a well known adventurer and explorer and has made numerous attempts at ballooning and sailing records, most successfully when his hot air balloon Virgin Atlantic Flyer crossed the Atlantic in 1987. This was, then, the largest balloon at 2.3 million cubic feet (65,000 m³), and the first hot-air balloon crossing of the Atlantic.

Media and property tycoon **Richard Desmond** (b. 1951) is reported to be worth £1,900 million. His first foray into the publishing world happened in 1974 when he purchased *International Musician and Recording World*. In 1993 *OK!* magazine was launched.

In 2000 Desmond purchased Express Newspapers for £125 million, which gave him control of four major UK newspapers; the *Daily Express*, the *Sunday Express*, the *Daily Star* and the *Daily Star Sunday*.

On March 19th 2008, Express Newspapers were forced to pay the parents of missing four-year-old Madeleine McCann £550,000 damages and publish a humiliating apology on the front pages of his four newspapers after publishing more than 100 defamatory articles about the couple.

Richard Livingstone, and his brother, Ian, have made their £1,880 million fortune through property development, particularly in Europe, and are owners of the London and

Regional Group. In 2007 the Livingstones secured the largest development deal in the world: a $7 billion (£3.5 billion) district in Panama City. The site is over 2,750 acres and will take 40 years to redevelop.

The company bought and redeveloped the old Marks and Spencer's head office in Baker Street, London, into its own headquarters at a cost of £210 million. The site is now reported to be worth £600 million.

In 1987 former scrap yard labourer **Richard Elman** founded the commodities supply company, Noble Group, in Hong Kong. The company's biggest market is the developing People's Republic of China, to which it supplies iron ore, steel, coal and other basics. The fortune of this self-confessed failure at school is £637 million.

Richard Caring has made much of his £450 million fortune through supplying clothes to high street retailers, such as Marks and Spencer and Next. His business breakthrough was to use Far-Eastern labour to maximise profits.

In 2004 he gained control of London's Camden Market for around £40 million. He has recently bought The Ivy and Le Caprice restaurants and paid £130 million for Wentworth golf course. He once forked out £190,000 at a charity auction to have dinner with Elton John.

Richard De Vos (b. 1926) is an American businessman who co-founded Amway in 1963 with his close friend, Jay Van Andel. The company became successful through the network marketing and selling of one multi-purpose cleaning product, although it later expanded its product range.

De Vos is a devout Christian and tries to promote the values of his religious beliefs in his business dealings. In 1994 he published *Compassionate Capitalism*, and has donated over £200 million of his £4,500 million fortune to health, education and the arts.

In 2004 he bought the Orlando Magics basketball team.

Born in 1732 and the youngest of 13 children, **Richard Arkwright** became one of the richest men in the world and known as one of the fathers of the Industrial Revolution. He is credited, alongside watchmaker John Kay, with inventing the water frame for spinning cotton.

In 1771, Arkwright and his colleagues established a spinning and weaving factory on the banks of the River Derwent at Cromford, Derbyshire. The venture made him a huge fortune and at his death he was found to be worth more than £500,000 – more than £28,000 million when converted to today's money.

Although he began his working life as a barber and wig-maker he was later to develop the modern industrial factory system. He was knighted in 1786.

US banker and industrialist **Richard B. Mellon** amassed a great fortune in the early 20th century thanks to his family's association with Gulf Oil. His worth when adjusted to current values was reckoned to be in the region of £43,000 million.

While working as a station agent for the US railroad in 1886, **Richard Warren Sears** began selling watches to others along the railway. His business soon took off and he had made $5,000 within six months.

The following year he moved to Chicago and hired Alvah Roebuck as his watch repairman. The pair founded the Sears-Roebuck mail order catalogue in 1893, with Sears writing most of the product copy. He is considered to be one of the great American promotional geniuses.

By 1897 the catalogue had expanded to 500 pages and was distributed to around 300,000 homes. Sears concentrated his efforts in rural areas near railway stations. He had grown up in the country and knew the frustrations of trying to shop for quality goods in small towns. His fortune (adjusted) was around £4,500 million.

He died of Bright's disease (a kidney infection noted by **Richard Bright** in 1827. Symptoms include severe back pain, vomiting and a high fever) aged 50, in 1914.

RIPENED RICHARDS

H. Richard Landis was a US veteran of World War I. He enlisted in the US Army in October 1918 but didn't complete his basic training as the hostilities ended the following month. During his military service he was exposed to the Spanish flu virus, which killed 75 million worldwide that same year.

He died on February 4th 2008 aged 108.

Richard Tracey, 'Brother Dick', was a resident of Sturge Town, a Quaker community in Jamaica, and was reckoned to be still reading without his glasses aged 106.

Richard Eberhart was a prolific American poet who published more than a dozen collections of poetry. He taught at St Mark's School in Southborough, Massachusetts, where poet Robert Lowell was amongst his pupils.

In 1956 he was sent to San Francisco by the *New York Times* to write about the Beat poets. His published article helped to bring this literary group to national prominence, particularly Allen Ginsburg.

He won the Pulitzer Prize in 1966 for a book of his collected poems.

Eberhart died on June 9th 2005, aged 101.

Another American who lived to 101 was **Richard D. Mudd**. He died on May 22nd, 2002.

His grandfather was convicted for aiding John Wilkes Booth assassinate President Abraham Lincoln. He spent much of his life trying to clear his grandfather's name.

Canadian politician **Richard G. Reid** also reached 101. He was the 7th premier of Alberta. He emigrated to Canada in 1903 after serving in the Boer War from 1900 to 1902. He was a Lance-Corporal in the Royal Army Medical Corps.

Richard Savage is a hundred-year-old native of Chicago, Illinois. A lifelong Chicago Cubs fan, he jokes that he has spent a century waiting for his favourite team to win the World Series. To date they still have not. Born in 1908, Savage has recently celebrated his centenary, at the time of writing.

In an interview with ESPN in September, 2008, he talks about the strength of character that fans of failing teams must have.

The UK's oldest career criminal is **Richard Blaylock** who has spent 42 years in jail. His first sentence began in 1943 when he was 11. He was apprehended by police in Carlisle while bungling his latest robbery.

When Blaylock was searched the officers found two screwdrivers, a chisel, a gas burner, a knife, a set of batteries, a torch and a magnifying glass (for his poor eyesight).

SOME CLEVER DICKS

British ethologist and evolutionary biologist **Richard Dawkins** (b.1941) is also a popular science writer and opinion maker. He first came to prominence with his book *The Selfish Gene* (1976) in which he argues the case for the evolutionary development of species based on natural selection.

For Dawkins the gene is the fundamental unit of evolution. He also coined the term *meme*, which is the cultural equivalent of a gene and outlined his theory that Darwinian principles may be used to explain the spread of ideas and cultural phenomena.

Dawkins is also renowned for his criticism of Creationism and Intelligent Design, ideas he refutes in his book *The Blind Watchmaker* (1986). He damns these notions as 'preposterous, mind-shrinking falsehood', and has spent a great deal of his life committed to exploding these myths.

He has been called 'Darwin's Rottweiler', because of his strong views on natural selection.

His most successful book, *The God Delusion* (2006), has sold more than 1½ million copies worldwide and has been translated into 31 languages.

In 2006 Dawkins formed the Richard Dawkins Foundation for Science and Reason to finance research on the psychology of belief and religion.

He is also a strong supporter of the Great Apes Project, which advocates a United Nations Declaration of the Rights of Great Apes that would confer basic legal rights on non-human great apes: chimpanzees, bonobos, gorillas, and orang-utans. The rights suggested are the right to life, the protection of individual liberty, and the prohibition of torture.

Richard Dixon Oldham was an Irish geologist who argued in 1906 that the Earth's core must be molten because seismic waves were not able to travel as quickly through liquids.

Richard Stanihurst was born in Dublin in 1547 and was known as a poet, historian and alchemist. In his treatise on alchemy, dedicated to King Phillip II of Spain, he claims to have witnessed 15 transmutations: of copper into silver 14 times, and of mercury into gold once.

American author **Richard H. Hall** has published books about the role of women in the American Civil War. He is also one of the United States' leading ufologists. Hall served as Chairman of the Fund for UFO Research from 1993 to 1998, and is the author of several books on the subject.

He is a strong proponent of the theory that UFOs are extraterrestrial spacecraft from an advanced alien civilization and his published works reflect this view. He is the editor of *The Journal of UFO Evidence*, which is published six times a year. His books include *Uninvited Guests* (1988) and two editions of *The UFO Evidence* (1964, revised and updated 2001).

A professor of linguistics at the University of West England in Bristol, **Richard Coates** is editor of *The Survey of English Place-Names* and is honorary director of the English Place-Name Society. He has offered a new etymology of London.

He believes it derives from Old European *(p)lowonida*, meaning 'boat river', or 'river too wide to ford', and suggests that this was a name given to the part of the River Thames which flows through London; from this, the settlement was named 'Lowonidonjon'.

Sir Richard Friend is Cavendish Professor for Physics at the University of Cambridge and has earned a world wide reputation for his research into the physics and engineering of carbon-based semiconductors.

Professor Friend's research is key to developing and producing truly flat panel displays, and future screens that can be rolled and transported. He has published more than 600 articles in support of this and has 20 patents on semiconductor technology.

In 2003 he was awarded the prestigious Faraday Medal by the Institute of Electrical Engineers and was knighted for 'services to physics'.

English scientist **Richard Caton** reported to the British Medical Association in 1875 that he had observed electrical impulses from the surface of living brains in animal subjects: 'The electric currents of the grey matter appear to have a relation to its functions.'

This work was crucial for Hans Berger to be able to discover Alpha wave activity in the human brain. This led to the systematic study of human brains with his development of the Electoencephalogram (EEG).

Richard Salisbury Ellis is Steele Professor of Astronomy at the California Institute of Technology (Caltech). He achieved his Doctorate at the University of Oxford, aged 24, and became a professor in 1985.

His work is primarily in observational cosmology, a branch of astronomy which considers the origin and evolution of galaxies, the evolution of large scale structures in the universe, and the nature and distribution of dark matter.

Particular interests include applications using gravitational lensing and high-redshift supernovae. His most recent discoveries relate to searches for the earliest known galaxies, seen when the universe was only a few per cent of its present age.

Richard J. C. Atkinson was a British archaeologist and pre-historian. He was from a Quaker family and served in non-combat roles during World War II. In 1944 he was appointed Assistant Keeper of Archaeology at Oxford's Ashmolean Museuem, where he produced a theory on the creation of Stonehenge and its possible uses.

In the 1940s he suggested that the site was built in three phases, begun around 2950BCE and completed around 1600BCE. He theorised that Stonhenge had been astronomically aligned to place significance on solstice and equinox points. It may have been used as a calendar with religious importance.

Between 1950 and 1964 he directed excavations at Stonehenge for the Ministry of Works. English Heritage holds over 2,000 of his pictures of the excavation in its archives. His book *Stonehenge* was published in 1956.

He was awarded the CBE in 1979.

Richard P. Feynman (1918-1988) was an American physicist known for his work on quantum mechanics, quantum electrodynamics and particle physics. He was a joint recipient of the Nobel Prize for Physics in 1965.

He was, like Albert Einstein, a late talker and apparently didn't utter a word until he was three. Einstein was later an attendee at Feynman's first seminar at Princeton University.

During World War II Feynman worked on the Manhattan Project, the USA's mission to build an atomic bomb. He was convinced of the necessity that the allied forces should have the super-weapon before the Nazis.

Feynman was a pioneer in quantum computing and introduced the world to ideas of nanotechnology – machinery that could be made on the molecular level. It was his contention that small components could be assembled together like Lego to make machines.

Alongside his scientific career, Feynman was also keenly interested in the arts and music. His art featured in an exhibition using his pseudonym, 'Ofey'. He loved to play the bongos and earned the nick-name 'Injun Joe', for his secret drumming during the Manhattan Project.

He also loved to play pranks on his colleagues and developed an aptitude for picking locks. His friend and fellow scientist, Freeman Dyson, called Feynman, 'half-genius, half-buffoon'. He later changed this to, 'all-genius, all-buffoon'.

Feynman's picture, along with a series of his famous diagrams, appeared on a commemorative stamp issued in the US in May, 2005.

British mathematician **Richard Q. Twiss** (1920-2005) initially made contributions to the theory of radar and basic electronics. In 1954, working with astronomer, Robert Hanbury-Brown, Twiss invented the optical intensity interferometer – a device which allowed scientists to measure the temperature of stars.

Richard S. Lazarus was an American psychologist who rose to prominence in the 1960s. He worked against the beliefs propounded by such behaviourists as B. F. Skinner, who suggested that all human actions could be explained as a result of basic motivations like reward or punishment.

Dr. Lazarus was a professor in the Department of Psychology at the University of California, Berkley, who was named by *American Psychologist* as one of the most influential in the field. He was a pioneer in the study of emotion and stress, especially their relation to cognition.

British palaeontologist **Richard Fortey** (b. 1946) claims he found his first fossilised trilobite aged 12, which led him into a long career at the Natural History Museum.

His books:

- *The Hidden Landscape* (1993) was named the Natural World Book of the Year.
- *Life: A Natural History of the First Four Billion Years of Life on Earth* (1997)
- *The Earth: An Intimate History* (2004)
- *Dry Store Room No 1: The Secret Life of the Natural History Museum* (2008)

He is a keen populariser of science and was Collier Professor for the Public Understanding of Science and Technology at the Institute of Advanced Studies in 2002.

He has won the Lewis Thomas Prize for science writing (2003) and was the 2006 holder of the Royal Society's Michael Faraday Prize for the public communication of science.

INVENTING RICHARDS

American inventor **Richard Gurley Drew** worked for the industrial giant 3M Company in St Paul, Minnesota from 1923. He is credited with inventing masking tape in 1925, whilst finding a solution to the problem of applying two bordering colours close together, for a car spraying workshop.

Unfortunately, the tape only had adhesive down its edge and the trial failed as the tape fell off the car during spraying. The workshop owner sent Gurley Drew away with the comment; "Tell your Scotch owners to put more adhesive on it."

By 'Scotch' the owner meant penny-pinching. The tape was re-developed and the nickname stuck.

In 1930 he invented the world's first transparent cellophane sticky tape, which was called *Sellotape* in the UK.

Whilst working on a meter to monitor power usage on US naval warships, **Richard T. James** knocked one of his long tension springs to the ground and noticed how it kept moving after it hit the floor. His idea to develop this into a toy became the Slinky.

He and his wife, Betty, borrowed $500 and manufactured 400 of the toys, which they were allowed to demonstrate at Gimbel's Department Store in Philadelpia during the Christmas season of 1945.

They sold all of their toys within 90 minutes.

In the 1960s James moved to Bolivia to join an evangelical religious sect and left the company to his wife. He died in 1974, aged 60. To date more than 300 million Slinkys have been sold.

The Slinky (under House Bill No.1893 – Session 2001, of the General Assembly of Pennsylvania) has been named the Official State Toy of Pennsylvania as of November 4th 2001.

(In 2003, James Industries merged with Poof Products!!!)

In 1924 an American electrical engineer, **Richard Howland Ranger**, invented the world's first wireless photoradiogram, or transoceanic radio facsimile, the forerunner to a machine we routinely call a 'fax' today.

The first picture was of President Calvin Coolidge and was broadcast from New York to London on November 29th and Ranger's invention went into production two years later.

After World War II Ranger was given access to German electronics technology whilst working for the US government and realised the far-reaching applications of magnetic tape recorders, particularly for musical use.

He demonstrated his refined machine to potential users, including the members of the Institute of Radio Engineers, the National Broadcasting Company, the

Radio Corporation of America, the American Institute of Electrical Engineers, and individuals like singer Bing Crosby.

His later work improved the synchronisation of the sound and visual elements of films, for which he was awarded an Oscar in 1956.

Dr. Richard Jordan Gatling was an American inventor best known for his invention of the Gatling gun, the first successful machine gun.

ARTISTIC RICHARDS

American photographer **Richard Avedon** made his reputation as a fashion photographer for *Harper's Bazaar* and *Vogue*. His famous photographs include; *Dovima with Elephants*, 1955, *Marilyn Monroe, actress*, 1957, *Dwight David Eisenhower, President of the United States*, 1964, *The Beatles*, 1967, *Andy Warhol and Members of the Factory*, New York 1969, and *Pile of beautiful people*, Versace campaign 1982.

Richard Estes is an American painter who is best known for his photo-realistic paintings. The paintings generally consist of reflective, clean, and inanimate city and geometric landscapes. He is regarded as one of the founders of the international photo-realist movement of the late 1960s, with painters such as Ralph Goings, Chuck Close, and Duane Hanson.

Richard Deacon is a British abstract sculptor, and a winner of the Turner Prize. He was awarded the CBE in 1999.

Richard Hamilton (b.1922) is a prolific English painter known for his contributions to the Pop Art movement. He left school with no formal qualifications but discovered a talent for draughtsmanship during an electrical apprenticeship. He took painting classes in the evenings and later entered the Royal Academy.

In the 1960s he became friends with Paul McCartney, an association which led to his cover design for the Beatles' White Album (1968). The collage of photos inside is also Hamilton's work.

His most famous painting, *Just What Is It that Makes Today's Homes So Different, So Appealing?* (1956) hangs in Kunsthalle Tübingen, Tubingen, Germany.

In 1957 he gave a definition of Pop Art as: "popular, transient, expendable, low-cost, mass-produced, young, witty, sexy, gimmicky, glamorous, and Big Business."

Richard Wilson (1713-1782) was a landscape painter from Montgomeryshire in Wales. He struggled to find success in his own lifetime, although later painters, such as Constable and Turner, cited his work as an influence.

Late in his life a student brought Wilson a wealthy lady client who commissioned the artist to paint her two landscapes. Wilson accepted the commission but admitted to his pupil that he couldn't afford to buy the canvases or paints. The student lent him £20 and immediately gave up any aspirations of becoming a professional painter himself, declaring; "When Wilson with all his genius starves, then what will become of me?"

Richard Long (b.1945) uses a mixture of painting, sculpture and photography to make representations of the landscapes he has walked in and has been nominated for the Turner Prize four times, winning the competition in 1989.

He has published two books about his artistic journeys; *Walking in Circles* (1991) and *Walking the Line* (2002) and in 2001 was elected a member of the Royal Academy.

Born in 1939, **Richard Serra** is a controversial sculptor known for his large scale steel monoliths placed in public spaces. His most famous work is *Tilted Arc* (1981), a giant curved wall of rusting steel dividing the Federal Office Plaza in New York. The installation met with complaints from the public and government officials, who argued that the piece presented a menace to personal and national security.

Serra is keen to argue that sculpture should be site specific and that, "to remove the work is to destroy it".

In the case of *Tilted Arc*, however, public outcry overcame the artistic imperative and the wall was removed in 1989.

ROYAL RICHARDS

Although King of England for ten years **Richard I** (1157-1199), or The Lionheart, only spent six months of his reign in the country. He was a member of the French Plantagenet family and spoke little English.

Richard spent most of his life in battle. His early campaigns were against his father, Henry II, in France. After his accession to the throne in 1189, he used his newly bestowed powers to raise taxes to finance a crusade. He took 8,000 men in a fleet of 100 ships to the Holy Land.

In 1191 he had 2,700 Muslim prisoners, held as hostages against Saladin, executed. He subsequently defeated Saladin at the Battle of Arsuf on September 7th 1191.

Realising that he could not hold Jerusalem if he took it, Richard decided to retreat. Whilst making his journey home he was shipwrecked and attempted to return to France over land.

Travelling disguised as a poor pilgrim – recognised because of his aristocratic taste for roast chicken – he was captured and imprisoned by Leopold V of Austria in December 1192, who demanded a high ransom.

He received thirty tons of gold for the king's release.

While campaigning in France in his later years Richard was shot by a crossbowman. The assailant was a young boy who claimed that Richard had killed his father. Richard forgave him as an act of mercy but after the king died from his gangrenous wound the boy was skinned alive and hanged by Richard's mercenary ally, Mercadier.

The Royal shield bearing three lions was introduced by Richard I.

Richard II (1367-1400) succeeded to the throne in 1377, aged 10. He was tutored by John of Gaunt for most of his years as a minor.

He first enters historical note during the Peasant's Revolt of 1381. After a series of punitive poll taxes, rebels led by Wat Tyler demanded an abolition of serfdom. By early June marauding mobs had burned down John of Gaunt's Savoy Palace and murdered the chancellor and the treasurer.

On June 14th, and realising that negotiation was the only way to secure peace, Richard met Tyler and agreed to his demands. The rebels, however, continued their looting and killing. When Richard met Tyler again the next day, William Walworth, the Mayor of London, enraged, pulled Tyler from his horse and killed him. Richard calmed the situation by calling out, "I am your captain, follow me", and led the rebel mob away from further trouble.

Richard assumed full control of government in 1389 and presided over an uneasy peace of eight years. Seven years later he agreed a 28-year truce with France. One of the conditions was his marriage to Isabella, daughter of Charles VI. She was seven years old.

In 1399 Henry Bolingbroke, son of John of Gaunt, came from France to depose Richard, who ruled with absolute authority. Richard surrendered to Henry and was imprisoned in the Tower of London, where Henry let him starve to death. His body was displayed at the old St. Paul's Cathedral.

The defeat of **Richard III** at the Battle of Bosworth by Henry Tudor in August, 1485 marked the end of the Plantagenet dynasty which had ruled England since Henry II took power in 1154.

Richard was the last king from the House of York.

Before usurping the throne in 1483 Richard had been a loyal servant of his brother, Edward IV, and had been on many campaigns in his support. In 1482 he recaptured Berwick-upon-Tweed from the Scots and is known to have been a keen patron of education.

However, when Edward died, Richard seized upon the opportunity to declare his marriage illegitimate and therefore Edward's sons, Edward V and Richard of Shrewsbury, had no claim to England. A Parliamentary decree supported Richard's action. The young princes were taken to the Tower of London and it is thought that they died there in 1483.

There is controversy amongst historians of the period as to whether Richard was responsible for the deaths of his nephews.

Much is made about Richard's fitness to rule and there have since been claims that he was a bad king. This was popularised by Shakespeare's portrayal of Richard, itself based upon the history of Thomas More, a notorious Tudor propagandist. Succeeding Tudor monarchs were happy to have Richard made famous for his physical deformities, which were supposed to be reflective of an evil nature.

In the last century there have been a number of societies set up to try and rehabilitate Richard's poor reputation, such as The Richard III Society, which has as its president, **Richard**, the current **Duke of Gloucester**.

The Society of the Friends of Richard III is another organisation attempting to recover Richard.

TV RICHARDS

Along with his partner, Ian La Frenais, **Dick Clement** (b. 1937) is one of the most successful and highly regarded TV screenwriters in Britain. Their list of popular sitcoms includes:

The Likely Lads (1964-66)
Whatever Happened to the Likely Lads? (1973-74)
Porridge (1974-77)
Auf Wiedersehen Pet (1983-84)

Clement also scripted the short-lived series *Going Straight* (1978) which followed the exploits of Norman Stanley Fletcher, the central character in *Porridge*, played by Ronnie Barker.

Clement also directed some of the cinema adaptations of their small screen hits. He provided the screenplay for *The Commitments* (1991).

TV presenter **Richard Hammond** (b. 1969) – or 'Hamster' as he is otherwise known by his co-presenters – is one of the regular trio who front BBC2's *Top Gear*. He joined the team, which also includes Jeremy Clarkson and James May, in 2002.

In September 2006, while filming for the series, Hammond was involved in a high speed car crash, in which he was seriously injured and hospitalised, while he was driving a jet powered car at 288mph.

The crash and Hammond's subsequent recovery were highly publicised but by December 2006 he was back at work and filming for the new series of *Top Gear*. He was presented with a Lego model of the Vampire car he crashed.

In July 2005 he was voted top of a poll in *Heat* magazine to determine weird celebrity crushes. In late 2007 Hammond recorded the last interview with American stuntman Evel Knievel. It was broadcast shortly after his death in November.

Richard Baker was a newsreader for the BBC from 1954 to 1982 and was the first person to read the news on TV for the BBC. Initially, presenters did not appear on screen but were hidden behind pictures. Baker has said of the BBC's attitude: "We were not to be seen reading the news because it was feared we might sully the pure stream of truth with inappropriate facial expressions, or (unthinkably) turn the news into a personality performance."

However, by 1956 Baker, and his colleague Robert Dougall, had been chosen as the regular hosts of the BBC's television news.

Baker introduced *The Last Night of the Proms* from the Royal Albert Hall for the BBC for 32 years.

He was the narrator for the children's cartoon *Mary, Mungo and Midge* in 1969 and ten years later was awarded the OBE. He was Newscaster of the Year three times.

Famous for his garish ties and jackets, **Richard Whiteley** (1943-2005) was presenter of Channel 4's *Countdown* for 23 years. The launch programme when Channel 4 began broadcasting at 4.45pm on November 2nd 1982, the first show attracted 3.5 million viewers, dropping to only 500,000 for the next edition.

However, *Countdown* grew steadily in popularity and, towards the end of Whiteley's era, audiences of four million were common.

At the time of his death Whiteley was believed to have clocked up more hours on British television screens – and more than 10,000 appearances – than anyone else alive, apart from the young girl who appeared on the BBC's iconic Test Card F.

Whiteley was also famous for being bitten by a ferret on a live TV show. The animal sank its teeth into his finger and wouldn't let go for over half a minute. The clip is still shown on TV out-takes programmes more than 30 years later.

He was taught English at school by the late TV chat show host Russell Harty.

In 2004 he was awarded the OBE for services to broadcasting.

Richard Madeley (b. 1956) is one half of TV duo Richard and Judy. He began his TV career as a co-presenter on Yorkshire TV's *Calendar* programme with namesake

Whiteley. He moved to Granada TV in the 1980s and met his co-presenter and (later) wife Judy Finnegan, eight years his senior, on his first day. The couple were married in 1986.

From 1988 to 2001 they presented ITV's *This Morning* magazine show. The pair were so closely associated with the show that it was generally referred to as 'Richard and Judy', rather than by its official title.

They quit their two-hour morning show for a one-hour early evening spot on Channel 4. The show was famous for its Richard and Judy Book Club and Richard and Judy Wine Club.

They broadcast their last show for Channel 4 on August 22nd 2008 and began their contract for UKTV's new channel, Watch, shortly after.

Richard Keys (b. 1957) started his sports broadcasting career in 1983 when he co-hosted ITV's *TV-am* with Anne Diamond.

In 1992 he moved to Sky Sports and became the anchor for the channel's Premiership football coverage, specialising in *Super Sunday*, Sky's presentation of that week's Sunday matches. He has presented more live football than any other broadcaster, covering over 800 matches, and also worked the longest on-screen shift.

In November 1996 he hosted coverage of England's World Cup qualification match against Georgia, which was followed by four consecutive world title fights, including Evander Holyfield's victory over Mike Tyson. He was in front of the camera for 18 hours.

Richard Bacon joined BBC TV's *Blue Peter* programme in February, 1997. Less than 18 months later he had his contract terminated after a report was published in the *News of the World* about him taking cocaine.

Since his sacking his media career has gone from strength to strength and he has presented *The Big Breakfast*, amongst others. He has regular shows on Capital FM, XFM and Radio 5 Live.

He says that his favourite piece of clothing would be one of his many cardigans, which would be one the first things he would save if his house caught fire.

He caused The Magic Numbers to walk off their scheduled *Top of the Pops* performance when he said that the band had been put in a 'fat melting pot of talent'.

Famous for the white streak running through his otherwise black hair, **Dickie Davies** (b. 1933) presented ITV's *World of Sport* from 1968 to 1985. He began his broadcasting career as Richard Davies but changed to Dickie on the advice of Jimmy Hill.

He is most proud of ITV's coverage of the 1980 Olympics in Moscow. He presented every show of the games' run.

Davies was often the target of TV impressionists, like Mike Yarwood, and has appeared, almost always as himself, on *Mind Your Language*, *The New Statesman*, and *Ant and Dec's Saturday Night Takeaway.*

Eric Morecambe appeared as a guest on the Christmas Eve edition of *World of Sport* in 1977 and caused mayhem by entertaining and trying to disrupt his friend Dickie's presentation links.

The Liverpool group, Half-man, Half-biscuit, released a parody of Kim Carnes's song Bette Davis Eyes, re-titled Dickie Davies Eyes, in 1986.

Richard McCourt is better known as the Dick of *Dick and Dom in da Bungalow*, which ran on BBC for 266 episodes from 2001 to 2006. In 2005 the programme was debated in Parliament when Conservative MP, Peter Luff, attacked it for its 'lavatorial' content.

They currently present *Are You Smarter than a Ten Year Old?* on Sky One.

Lieutenant-Colonel **Richard Francis 'Dick' Strawbridge** MBE is a British engineer, television presenter and environmentalist. He is often referred to as 'Colonel Dick'. He is most famous for his appearances on Channels 4's *Scrapheap Challenge.*

In 2006 he and his family were featured in the BBC 2 Series *It's Not Easy Being Green,* which challenged them to live an ecologically sound lifestyle without making too many sacrifices to achieve their goal.

Strawbridge said, "I don't want to wear a hemp shirt and hairy knickers, I want a 21st-century lifestyle with a coffee machine."

Richard Whitmore was a newsreader for the BBC, beginning his career in 1973 when he was chosen as an anchorman for the first version of *The Nine O'Clock News.* For the next 15 years he appeared on most major news programmes.

He famously appeared (along with other presenters and newsreaders) in the 'Nothing Like a Dame' musical number on the *Morecambe and Wise Christmas Show* in 1977, which was watched by over 29 million viewers and is still featured in highlights compilations of the comedy duo's show.

SPORTING RICHARDS

Football

Republic of Ireland central defender Risteárd Ó Duinn (**Richard Dunne**) made his professional debut for Everton aged 16 in 1996. He played 60 games for the Merseyside club before being transferred to Manchester City for £3 million in 2000.

Dunne first won the Player of the Year award for the 2004/05 season and has subsequently won it every season since, making him the first Manchester City player to win the accolade four times.

He has been club captain since July 2006.

Richard Gough began his footballing career at Dundee United in 1980. He played 165 games, scoring 23 goals, and helped the club to win the Scottish title in 1982/83.

In 1986 he moved south to play for Tottenham Hotspur but returned to Scotland the following season as he missed his home country. When Rangers bought him in 1987 he became Scotland's first £1 million player.

Gough stayed at Rangers until 1997 and played 318 games for the Glasgow side. He captained the Blues to a record nine consecutive Scottish League titles and is still the only Rangers player to have nine winner's medals.

He played two seasons in US Major League Soccer and returned to the UK to play for his former Rangers manager, Walter Smith, at Everton, where he finished his playing career in 2001.

He won 61 caps for Scotland but his international career was ended prematurely after he was openly critical of coaches Andy Roxburgh and Craig Brown and withdrew himself from further selection.

Goalkeeper **Richard Wright** (b. 1977) made his debut for Ipswich Town in a defeat against Manchester City in 1996. He played 293 league and cup games for Ipswich and was promoted with the Suffolk club after the 1999/2000 season.

He was transferred to Arsenal in 2001 for £6 million. Whilst there, he slipped to third choice keeper and only played 22 times for the Gunners. Although he rarely played he still qualified for a medal when Arsenal won the Premier League title in 2001/02.

He has won two caps for England but hasn't been part of the squad since 2003.

Richard Shaw (b. 1968) started his playing career at Crystal Palace in 1986 and made 207 appearances for the south London club. He played in the 1990 FA Cup Final, which Palace drew with Manchester United 3-3. United won the replay 1-0.

In 1995 Shaw was again playing for Palace against Manchester United and was given the task of marking Eric Cantona. He was so effective that he kept Cantona out of the game and the Frenchman showed his frustration by taking a kick at Shaw. Cantona was sent off and as he marched to the dressing room he launched his infamous kung-fu kick at Palace supporter, Matthew Simmons.

Shaw has won the Player of the Year award at all three of his clubs; Crystal Palace in 1995, Coventry City in 1999 and Millwall in 2007.

Rugby

Born in Rugby in 1970, the birthplace of Webb-Ellis's game, **Richard Cockerill** played as a hooker for Leicester Tigers. He won 27 caps for England and famously stood eyeball-close to New Zealand's Norm Hewitt while the All Blacks were performing their pre-match haka at Old Trafford in 1997.

He published his autobiography *In Your Face: a Rugby Odyssey* in 1999. The cover picture features his staring match with Hewitt. He was openly critical of England coach Clive Woodward in his book and was subsequently dropped from the team.

Flanker **Richard Hill** played club rugby for Saracens and earned 71 caps for England during a long and distinguished career, which peaked when he was a part of the 2003 World

Cup winning side. He is one of the most highly regarded flankers in world rugby and noted for his 'silent assassin' approach to the game.

He is the only player never to have been dropped during Sir Clive Woodward's England tenure.

Hill's man-of-the-match performance in the Heineken Cup victory over Ospreys in April 2008 came despite playing through injury. He played his last game for Saracens in May 2008.

Nicknamed 'The Enforcer', New Zealand prop forward **Richard Loe** played 49 tests for the All Blacks between 1987 and 1995. He made 18 World Cup appearances in the Silver Fern shirt and was part of the winning side in 1987.

Richard Wigglesworth plays at scrum-half for Sale Sharks in the Guinness Premiership. He was called up to the England team for the Six Nations Championships in 2008, and scored a try against France in the 24-13 victory in Paris. It was his first start for his country.

All Black number 1014, **Richard 'Richie' McCaw** (b. 1980) began his international career in 2001. He is captain of the Kiwis and was promoted to the position aged just 23. In 2006 he was the International Rugby Board Player of the Year.

Olympics

Richard Sheldon competed at the 1900 summer Olympics for the USA and won the gold medal for the shot-put and bronze for the discus.

At the 1912 summer games in Stockholm, American **Richard Byrd** competed in the standing high jump event and finished fourth. In the standing long jump competition he finished eighth. He also participated in the two handed discus – winning silver – throw event and finished 17th. None of these events are a part of the modern games.

Richard 'Dick' Fosbury (b. 1947) is the American athlete who revolutionised the world of high-jumping. At the 1968 summer games in Mexico City, Fosbury demonstrated his new, back first, technique, taking the gold medal and setting a new world record of 2.24m.

He was the only athlete using this method in Mexico. At the Munich games four years later 28 of the 40 athletes had converted to the 'Fosbury Flop'. In 1980 13 of the 16 finalists used the 'flop', and 34 of the 36 medallists between 1974 and 2006 used the method. It is still the most popular and effective high-jump technique.

Kenyan long distance runner **Richard Chelimo** (1971-2002) was involved in the controversial 10,000m final in Barcelona in 1992. On the last lap he was neck and neck with his title rival, Moroccan athlete, Khalid Skah.

The two athletes lapped another Moroccan runner who, contrary to the sporting code, kept pace with the tussling competitors. His interference meant that Skah won the race. He was quickly disqualified and Chelimo was awarded gold in his place. The next day, however, the Olympic officials reversed their decision after an appeal by the Moroccan team. At the medal ceremony the Spanish crowd loudly booed Skah and gave Chelimo a standing ovation.

Richard 'Torpedo' Thompson is a sprinter who competes for Trinidad and Tobago. At the 2008 Beijing games he won the silver medal in the 100m and the 4 x 100m relay. His performance was eclipsed by the Jamaican Usain Bolt.

British gold medal winners

Richard Faulds won the gold medal for the double-trap shooting event at Sydney, 2000.

Richard Gunn won the boxing featherweight gold at the 1908 games in London.

Richard McTaggart was a lightweight boxer who won a gold medal for the British team in 1956.

Richard Meade has won three gold medals for equestrian and team eventing. He won two team medals in the 1968 and 1972 Olympics and an individual gold in 1972.

Richard Dodds was captain of the British hockey team which took the gold medal at the Seoul games of 1988. The team also included **Richard Leman**.

Horseracing

Richard Johnson (b. 1977) has ridden more than a thousand winners in his career. He won the 2000 Tote Cheltenham Gold Cup with 'Looks Like Trouble' and the 2002 Queen Mother Champion Chase with 'Flagship Uberalles'.

He is the only jockey riding today to have won all four of the championship races at Cheltenham. He was in a five-year relationship with the Queen's grand-daughter, Zara Phillips, which created great media interest but ended in 2003.

In a career which lasted from 1979 to 2005, **Richard Hills** rode 1,832 winners.

At 5ft 10ins. **Richard Hughes** is the UK's tallest jockey. As of September 2003, Hughes had ridden 112 winners from 643 rides, earning prize money of £1,927,016.

Cricket

Richard 'Richie' Benaud's (b. 1930) dual careers playing cricket and in broadcasting have led to him becoming one of the best known voices in the game. He has been described as 'perhaps the most influential cricketer and cricket personality since the Second World War'.

He played in 63 tests for Australia from 1952 to 1964 and captained his country 28 times. Australia never lost a Test series under Benaud's captaincy, which was noted for its positive playing style, tactical astuteness and his ability to get the best from his players.

A right-arm leg-spinner and right handed batsman, Benaud took 248 Test wickets, at an average of 27.03, and scored 2201 runs (including nine fifties and three centuries) with an average score of 24.45. Benaud was the first cricketer to reach the test landmark of 200 wickets and 2000 runs.

In a long commentary career for the BBC, Australia's Channel 9 and UK's Channel 4, Benaud was noted for his analytical and laid back presentation. His final UK commentary was for the 2005 Ashes series.

A 'free to view' champion, Benaud retired from UK commentary after BSkyB acquired the rights to show Test cricket on cable and satellite only.

Taking over the captaincy from Steve Waugh in 2004, **Ricky Ponting**, (b.1974) is renowned as 'the archetypal modern cricketer… and knows only to attack'.

He is the third highest ranked Test batsman of all time and has scored over ten thousand runs in over 119 Test matches at an average of nearly 60 runs. He is Australia's greatest-ever run scorer in One Day internationals, with over eleven thousand runs to his name from 298 matches.

Ponting is the greatest Australian centurion, with 34 (his first came against England at Headingley in 1997) and has scored the most runs on Australian soil.

Ponting was the first Australian captain since Allan Border in 1986-87 to lose an Ashes series. After losing the Edgbaston Test match in 2005 by 2 runs, Ponting said: "Although we lost it has been a great Test and one of the best I have ever played in."

Richard Benjamin 'Richie' Richardson (b. 1962) was part of the West Indies cricket team that dominated world cricket until the mid 1990s.

He would generally be seen walking out to open the batting wearing his trademark wide-brimmed maroon sunhat. Like his team-mate Viv Richards, Richardson declined to wear a helmet.

A flamboyant and 'destructively brilliant' right-handed batsman, Richardson played in 86 test matches for the

West Indies between 1983 and 1995. He scored 5,949 runs at an average of 44.39 and made 16 hundreds and 27 fifties.

He took over the captaincy of the West Indies from Viv Richards and nurtured the careers of the great West Indies bowling partnership Curtly Ambrose and Courtney Walsh.

Richardson is the captain of the Lashings XI celebrity cricket team.

Knighted for services to cricket in 1990, **Richard Hadlee** (b. 1951) is regarded as one of the greatest fast bowlers of all time and one of the quartet of great all-rounders from the 1980s, which included Imran Khan, Kapil Dev and Ian Botham.

The left-handed batsman and right-arm fast bowler played in 86 Test matches for New Zealand between 1973 and 1990. He scored 3,124 runs at an average of 27.16 and has a highest score of 151 not out. Hadlee took 431 wickets at an average of 22.29. His best bowling figures were 9 wickets for 52 runs and he was the first cricketer to pass the landmark of 400 test wickets.

He was part of the side which bowled out England for 64 in 1978 to secure the Kiwis' first test victory over 'the mother country'.

Richard Montgomerie (b. 1971) made his first class cricketing debut for Northamptonshire in 1991. He moved to Sussex in 1999 where he formed a successful opening partnership with Murray Goodwin. Their unbeaten 372 for the first wicket against Nottinghamshire in 2001 is still a record opening partnership.

He won the county championship with Sussex in 2003 and 2007 and was part of the double winning side of 2006.

Montgomerie retired from cricket at the end of the 2007 season to become a full-time teacher.

Possibly the most famous cricket umpire of the modern era, **Harold 'Dickie' Bird** (b. 1933) stood in 66 Test matches between 1973 and 1996, when he retired from international umpiring. On his final Test at Lords the two competing teams, England and India, formed a guard of honour and at the end of the match the emotional Yorkshireman was reduced to tears.

He played cricket in the same Barnsley team as Geoff Boycott and Michael Parkinson and, between 1956 and 1964, played county cricket for Yorkshire and Leicestershire. A right-handed batsman, Bird scored 3,314 runs with an average of 20.71. His highest score was 181 not out.

Known for his nervous tics in the middle, as well as his trademark white cap, Bird came to be highly regarded for top quality umpiring. He said: "They all rated me the best: Sobers, Richards, Lillee and Botham. That means a lot, I can tell you."

Awarded the MBE in 1986, he has been granted the freedom of Barnsley, where a six foot statue has been erected in his honour.

Cycling

French cyclist **Richard Virenque** was known as a climbing specialist and held the Tour de France's polka dot jersey as King of the Mountains an unequalled seven times.

In 1998 he was embroiled in the sports biggest doping scandal when his Festina team were accused of using the performance enhancing drug EPO. He was later cleared of this charge.

Speed

Richard Noble (b.1946) held the land speed record from 1983 to 1997 after reaching 633mph in his car Thrust 2.

He is planning another world record attempt in 2011 and aims to drive at over 1000mph in Bloodhound SSC. The car will be accelerated to 300mph by the engine of a Eurofighter aircraft and then reach top speed with a rocket booster specially designed for the project.

To practice for the record attempt Noble will fly upside down in stunt aircraft!

<u>Boxers</u>

Ricky 'The Hitman' Hatton is a two-time IBF and IBO Light Welterweight Champion. On May 24th 2008, Hatton beat Mexican Juan Lazcano by unanimous decision at the City of Manchester Stadium to retain *The Ring Magazine* and IBO light welterweight titles.

Dick Turpin was an English middleweight boxer. He contested 104 fights, winning 77 with 33 knockouts. He held the titles of British and Commonwealth champion in 1948.

Dick Curtis (1802-1843) was a bare-knuckle boxer who turned professional in 1820. He remained undefeated for eight years. He was defeated once, in 1828, by Jack Perkins.

Dick Corbett (Richard Coleman 1908-1943) was British bantamweight champion in 1932 and again in 1934. He won 131 of his 185 fights, 32 by knockout.

Heavyweight boxer **Richard Dunn** (b.1945) is remembered as the last opponent that Muhammad Ali knocked out; in round five of a bout in Munich in May, 1976. Dunn won 33 out of his 45 fights, 15 by KO.

Soapy Richards

EastEnders

EastEnders' put upon mechanic, **Ricky Butcher** is played by Sid Owen. The character first appeared in the BBC soap opera in May 1988 and is famous for his on-screen romance with Bianca Jackson.

The two characters first met in 1994 and their volatile relationship eventually led to marriage in 1997 – an episode watched by 22 million viewers.

Ricky returned for his third spell in Walford in March 2008.

Richard Cole was infamous as 'Tricky Dicky'. Played by Ian Reddington, Cole arrived as the new market inspector of Walford in 1992.

He was known for his 'sly, underhand and slimy' business dealings, brief flings with the women in the Square, and was an arch enemy of Ian Beale, who discovered that Cole had absconded with £40,000.

Cole enjoyed winding Beale up by hinting that he was having an affair with his wife – but the tryst never happened.

Actor **Richard Driscoll** played the troubled Reverend Alex Healy in *EastEnders* from 1997 to 1999. He had a long involvement with Kathy Beale (played by Gillian Taylforth) and considered leaving the Church to be with her.

His heart was broken when Kathy left the Square for South Africa.

PC **Richard Crewe** made only two appearances in the soap. In the first he was the community liaison officer at a meeting organised by Ian Beale.

In his second appearance he made an award to Dot Cotton for her part in foiling a burglary. He later noticed that Dot was making tea with cannabis and arrested her.

Other Soapy Richards

Richard A. Shapiro and his wife, Esther, are best known as the screenwriters of the long-running 1980s TV soap, *Dynasty*.

It ran for 220 episodes and gave the world Blake and Krystal Carrington, super-rich American oil barons. The second series introduced Joan Collins' character, the scheming Alexis Carrington.

Richard Hillman was a *Coronation Street* character played by Brian Capron.

Initially a charming con man, Hillman changed to become a fully-fledged serial killer. He murdered three

Street residents and attempted to kill his own wife and stepchildren. He was dubbed 'Killman Hillman' by the British press.

Hillman drowned when he drove his car and family into a local canal. His family escaped.

WRITING RICHARDS

Richard Bach is an American author and aviator. His most successful books were published in the 1970s.

Jonathan Livingston Seagull (1970) and *Illusion: Adventures of a Reluctant Messiah* (1977) were both huge best-sellers and espoused his philosophy that our apparent physical limits and mortality are merely appearance.

The first book is an allegorical tale about a seagull who did not want to accept the limits imposed on him by nature and society. According to an article in *People Magazine* from 1992, the book has sold more than 30 million copies.

It has been made into a film, a ballet, an audio book read by Richard Harris, endless parodies, and is listed as one of 50 'spiritual classics' in a book by Tom Butler-Bowdon.

Illusions sold over 15 million copies.

Richard Wright was an African-American author. His work helped redefine discussions of race relations in America in the mid-20th century.

He first gained national attention for the collection of four short stories titled *Uncle Tom's Children* (1938). He based some stories on lynching in the Deep South.

The successful sales of the book, combined with a Guggenheim fellowship, allowed Wright the financial freedom to write his most important novel, *Native Son* (1940).

The central character, Bigger Thomas, was in the top 20 of a list of the 100 Best Characters in Fiction Since 1900, which appeared in *Book* magazine, in March/April 2002.

His autobiographical *Black Boy* was published in 1945.

Richard Adams (b. 1920) is an English writer best known for his 1972 novel *Watership Down*. The original story was based on a collection of tales that Adams told his daughters on family trips to the countryside. Although critical reviews were unfavourable the book became an international best-seller and has sold around 50 million copies to date, earning Adams more than all of his other books put together.

In *The Big Read*, a 2003 survey of the British public, it was voted the 42nd greatest book of all time. It was adapted for the cinema in a 1978 animated version. The theme song, Bright Eyes, was a number one hit in the UK for Art Garfunkel.

Adams's other books include; *Shardik* (1974), *The Plague Dogs* (1977) and *The Girl in a Swing* (1980).

Richard Suskind was a children's author who created a fraudulent autobiography of the reclusive billionaire Howard Hughes, with author Clifford Irving. Suskind was incarcerated for five months of a six-month prison sentence for his role in collaborating with Irving on the scam. He died in 1999.

He was portrayed in the 2007 film *The Hoax* by Alfred Molina.

Dick Francis (b.1920) is the son of a jockey and stable manager. He was a pilot in World War II and flew both fighter and bomber aircraft, including the Spitfire.

He was a successful jockey in his own right. After leaving the RAF in 1946 he won over 350 races, becoming champion jockey in the 1953-54 season. From 1953 to 1957 he was jockey to Queen Elizabeth the Queen Mother.

Francis is now more famous as a prolific author of crime fiction, generally set in the world of horse racing. He published *Dead Cert* in 1962 and has published a book a year since.

He has won the Mystery Writers of America's Edgar Award for Best Novel three times – the only author to do so. In 1976 he was given the Grand Master Award, the highest honour bestowed by the MWA.

Francis is the uncle of Leigh Francis, creator of *Bo' Selecta!*

Richard McClure Scarry (1919-1994) was a popular American children's author and illustrator who published over 300 books. His total book sales are over 300 million worldwide.

He is famous for his *Busytown* books, populated by anthropomorphised animals, such as Mr. Fixit, the fox, who works as a repairman. His characters are always shown in human occupations, driving cars and wearing clothes. During the 1960s he wrote a series of books about the adventures of two friends, Tinker and Tanker – a rabbit and a hippo.

Richard Doddridge 'R. D.' Blackmore was a Victorian romantic author in the style of Thomas Hardy. He was renowned for his attention to descriptive detail.

Although prolific and popular in his own lifetime his reputation today rests on *Lorna Doone* (1869). He reputedly wrote the novel to emulate the speech style of 17th century Devon.

Blackmore is reputed to have invented the name 'Lorna' for his heroine. Most of his other books are now out of print.

Playwright **Richard Brinsley Sheridan** was born in Ireland in 1751. His first play *The Rivals* was performed at Covent Garden in 1775 – the first night was a failure.

Sheridan replaced his lead actor and the play went on to become a great success gaining a reputation as a standard of English theatre. His most famous play *The School for*

Scandal (1777) is considered one of the greatest comedies of manners in English.

Sheridan's success allowed him to buy a theatre on Drury Lane from his contemporary David Garrick. The theatre burned down in 1809 and, when he was found to be drinking outside the blaze he said; "A man may surely be allowed to take a glass of wine by his own fireside."

Also a Whig politician, he entered Parliament in 1780 and was a great public speaker becoming an important figure in the party. He remained in Parliament until 1812.

Sheridan died in poverty in 1816 and his funeral was attended by many dukes and noblemen, including the Lord Mayor of London. He is buried in Poets' Corner at Westminster Abbey.

ARCHITECTURAL RICHARDS

Richard Cementarius (aka **Richard the Mason**) was a 13th century architect who became the first Provost of Aberdeen in 1272.

He was appointed *King's Master Mason* by King Alexander III of Scotland. It is thought that Cementarius designed the old tower of Drum Castle near Drumoak in Aberdeenshire, considered to be one of the oldest towers in Scotland.

He is known to be the architect of the nearby Brig o' Balgownie. Both contain elements which define his work, such as distinctive pointed arches.

Richard Grainger was a 19th century builder from Newcastle-upon-Tyne. He was crucial in the redevelopment of the town centre, which began in 1834. By the time of the completion the 12 acre site comprised the meat market, which contained 180 butchers, 9 streets, 10 inns, 12 public houses, 325 shops (with homes attached) and 40 private houses.

Grainger's legacy was the elegant Grey Street, which curves to the left as it heads downhill towards Dean Street. Part of the way down, the sweep is interrupted by the projecting portico – a structure consisting of a roof supported by columns or piers, usually attached to a building as a porch – of the Theatre Royal.

At the top of the road, Grainger placed the column of Grey's Monument as a focus for the whole scheme, which cost £646,000.

The eponymous Grainger Street and Grainger Market are part of an area referred to as Grainger Town where 40% of the buildings are listed as being of historical and architectural importance.

In 2005 Grey Street was voted England's finest street in a survey of BBC Radio 4 listeners.

Richard Cromwell Carpenter was a Victorian church architect. He championed the gradual drift away from the more classical style of 18th century building towards the Gothic style which was to typify the Victorian period.

He built St Paul's Parish Church in Brighton, which has been described as 'one of the first successful nineteenth-century Gothic buildings'. The building still has a full set of stained glass windows.

Perhaps Cromwell Carpenter's most notable work was Lancing College in West Sussex (1854). His work was so popular at the time that the college's founder, Nathaniel Woodard, described the great chapel as an 'immemorial creed in stone'.

Richard Shaw was the most influential and successful of all late Victorian architects in Great Britain. His buildings in London include the Savoy Theatre (1881), New Scotland Yard (1887 to 1907) and the Piccadilly Hotel, Picadilly Circus (1905 to 1908).

A Royal Academician from 1877, Shaw co-edited the 1892 collection of essays 'Architecture, a Profession or an Art?' He firmly believed that it was an art form.

Sir Richard Herbert Sheppard was a 20th century architect who specialised in academic buildings. His firm built secondary schools (over 80 of them), technical colleges and universities.

He has won many awards from the Royal Institute of British Architects including work for Loughborough, Imperial College, University of Durham, Cambridge and Brunel.

He was knighted in 1981 and died a year later, aged 72.

Richard George Rogers, Baron Rogers of Riverside (b. 1933) is a British architect noted for his work in Modernist and Functionalist design. After graduating from Yale School of Architecture he set up design agency Team 4 with Norman Foster.

Rogers' first building of international importance was the Pompidou Centre in Paris, which opened in 1978. According to his website, 'it has become the most visited building in Europe and continues to attract some seven million visitors a year, more than the Louvre and the Eiffel Tower combined'.

The Centre was initially controversial and was criticised for its 'inside- out' structure, a feature which gave rise to the term 'Bowellism'.

Based on the rationale that the greatest amount of floor space possible should be allowed for the interior so as to maximise space to appreciate the exhibitions, everything from the lifts to the sewage pipes were made visible on the outside of the structure.

He has since built such landmarks as Lloyd's building, London (1979-84), Millennium Dome, London (1999), The Senedd, the new building for the National Assembly for Wales, Cardiff (2006), and Heathrow Terminal 5, London (2008).

Rogers has been chosen as the architect of Tower 3 of the new World Trade Center in New York City, replacing the original building destroyed in the September 11th 2001 attacks.

His old classmate, contemporary and former practice partner Norman Foster is also designing a new tower.

REPROBATE RICHARDS

Richard DiNome was alleged to be a member of the New York crime syndicate the DeMeo Crew, which was affiliated with the Gambino family.

DiNome was an expert car thief and it is thought that he stole up to 70 cars a day. He would deliver the vehicles to his brother Frank's car workshop where they would be 'chopped', re-worked and sold on.

He was found murdered by a single gunshot wound to the back of his head on February 4th 1984. He was 29.

Richard 'The Iceman' Kuklinski (b. 1935) was a prolific assassin for the New York Mafia. His own claims about the number of deaths he was responsible for vary between 130 and 200.

He was recruited to the job of hitman by Roy DeMeo, a high ranking Gambino family mobster, to whom he owed money. It is reputed that DeMeo tested Kuklinski's suitability by choosing a random passer-by for him to kill.

Kuklinski calmly left DeMeo's side and shot the pedestrian in the back of the head. But his preferred method of dispatching his victims was by using cyanide.

He would often spike the victim's food, inject them or spray them with the substance. Detecting cyanide after death is difficult. He earned his nickname for his habit of freezing the bodies of his victims in order to confuse police about the time of death.

Kuklinski died in jail in 2006. He was due to testify against Mafia boss Sammy Gravone. After his death the charges against Gravone were dropped as they relied heavily on Kuklinski's evidence. The cause of his death remains a mystery.

Richard Town was executed for fraudulent bankruptcy on December 23rd 1712. He had been attempting to flee charges brought against him by taking a boat to Ostend.

He became seasick whilst aboard and, on moving to the side of the boat to vomit, dropped two bags containing 800 guineas he had concealed under his coat.

During a storm the boat was forced back to port and Town was arrested. He had managed to hold onto £20 of his creditors' money, which, when discovered, was taken as evidence of his guilt.

Richard 'Dick' Turpin (b. 1706) is famous as the legendary lone, dashing highwayman who robbed rich travellers across the south of England. The truth of his life is a little less romantic.

He trained as a butcher and, after opening his own shop began to steal lamb, sheep and cattle, which he butchered and sold on.

He became a member of the Essex Gang which specialised in robbing remote farmhouses but was also involved in many cases of burglary, theft and livestock rustling.

When investigations of the gang became too close for Turpin he ran away to Yorkshire where he lived under the assumed name of John Palmer.

During an argument with his landlord, Turpin shot the man's rooster and was eventually arrested and imprisoned. During his incarceration he wrote a letter to his brother asking him for a good character reference. His brother was too mean to pay the sixpence postage.

When the letter went back to the post office Turpin's handwriting was recognised. After a positive identification of him as Turpin, and not Palmer, he was sentenced to death.

He was executed in public at York racecourse on April 7th 1739.

Dick Hughes, a burglar and robber, was executed on June 24th 1709, aged 30. His wife bought the rope to hang him as a final display of love.

His body was used for anatomical dissection at Surgeons' Hall in London.

MORE MUSICAL RICHARDS

A long-time member of folk-rock group, Fairport
Convention, guitarist and singer, **Richard Thompson,**
has had a long and varied career as a solo musician. He
recorded six albums from 1973-82 with his then wife Linda,
and has collaborated with some of the most highly regarded
artists of the 1970s. He played guitar on Nick Drake's
albums Five Leaves Left and Bryter Layter. He also guested
on John Martyn's seminal record Solid Air, which was
dedicated to the chronically depressed Drake.

Disillusioned with the music industry, Thompson retired to
a Sufi commune in East Anglia in 1975. He is still a devoted
Muslim.

Thompson appeared in Rolling Stone magazine's top twenty
guitarists of all time. A tribute album, Beat the Retreat,
features his songs being covered by REM, David Byrne and
The Blind Boys of Alabama. It was released in 1994.

He continues to write and record music and constantly
tours in Europe and North America. His latest album,
Sweet Warrior, was released in 2007. It was self-financed
and licensed to various record labels for distribution.

American musician James Ambrose Johnson Jr. is better
known as **Rick James**, the self-styled King of Punk-Funk.

His first band, The Mynah Birds, was formed in 1964
after James had escaped to Canada, fleeing the US Naval

Reserve. An early line-up of the band included Neil Young on guitar. The Mynah Birds recorded an album for Motown but it was shelved after their manager stole the advance money.

After his band folded James became a songwriter and producer for Motown and worked with Smokey Robinson and other label-mates under an assumed name.

In 1977 James formed the Stone City Band and experimented with a mix of musical styles he dubbed 'funk n roll'. It was this music which caught the ear of Motown impresario Berry Gordy. And in 1978 James' solo album, Come Get It, was released. His 1981 long-player, Street Songs, included the hit Super Freak, which was later sampled by MC Hammer for his worldwide smash hit U Can't Touch This. James sued Hammer and the two made an out-of-court settlement which included crediting James as a co-songwriter.

James produced Eddie Murphy's debut single Party All the Time, which reached number two in the US Billboard chart. It was also voted number sevn in VH1's The 50 Most Awesomely Bad Songs Ever.

In 1993 James was convicted of assaulting two women, one of whom he and his wife held hostage for six days whilst on a crock cocaine binge.

A documentary of his life, *I'm Rick James*, was released in 2007.

Richard Cole was tour manager for rock and roll giants Led Zeppelin from 1968 to 1970 after having had a stint organising road trips for The Who.

Cole was the first manager to implement the practice of shipping all of a band's equipment and crew on tours, previously all bands had hired their gear and crew. He is also given responsibility for introducing Led Zep to groupies he had met while on tour with other bands.

In May 1973 suspicion fell in Cole when more than $180,000 of the band's money disappeared from their New York hotel. Cole had the key to the safe deposit box. He was the first to discover the loss of the money but neither he nor anyone from the band was charged with the theft. The money was never recovered and Led Zeppelin later sued the hotel.

After being sacked from the band Cole was mistakenly imprisoned after a terrorist attack in Italy. While in prison he managed to overcome his heroin addiction. On release he was so broke he had to work as a scaffolder.

Cole has also tour managed Eric Clapton, Ozzy Osbourne and Black Sabbath.

His 1992 book *Stairway to Heaven*: *Led Zeppelin Uncensored* was slammed by the band as "permanently distorted". Jimmy Page even considered suing Cole. Despite this he was invited to the VIP area for the band's 2007 reunion concert.

Richard Coles is a classically trained pianist who found fame with Jimmy Somerville in 1980s pop group, The Communards. The band were together for two albums over three years and released nine top-ten singles. Their biggest hit was a cover of Don't Leave Me This Way, which stayed at number one in the UK for four weeks and was the biggest selling single of 1986.

After The Communards dissolved, Cole pursued a career in the Church of England and is currently curate of St. Botolph's in Boston, Lincolnshire.

Along with his partner Jerry Ross, **Richard Adler** was a composer of Broadway musicals in the 1950s. The duo's first success came in 1953 with Tony Bennett's number one recording of their song Rags to Riches. They wrote two hit shows, *The Pajama Game* (1954) and *Damn Yankees* (1955). Both shows have been revived on Broadway in recent years.

American guitarist and producer **Richard Podolor** has had a long and successful career. In the early 1960s, as **Richie Allen**, he was an architect of the southern Californian surf sound and recorded ten singles and three albums for Imperial Records.

He worked as a session guitarist and studio engineer for the Monkees, Electric Prunes and the Grateful Dead. But, it would be as a producer that Podolor would achieve his greatest successes.

Behind the desk for American rock band, Three Dog Night, Podolor recorded six albums, starting with It Ain't Easy in1970. This team yielded three number one hits, starting with Mama Told Me Not To Come, and culminating in Joy To The World, in 1971, which reached the top of the US Billboard Hot 100 and was the Billboard number one best-selling single of that year.

Jazz double-bass player, **Richard Davis,** has appeared on more than 2,000 recordings by a wide range of artists. He has performed with Jazz legends Miles Davis, Dizzy Gillespie, Chet Baker and Eric Dolphy.

Davis also played bass on Van Morrison's seminal album Astral Weeks (1968). According to producer Lewis Merenstein, Davis was pivotal during the session; "If you listen to the album, every tune is led by Richard and everybody followed Richard and Van's voice."

He appeared a guest on Bruce Springsteen's Born to Run (1975).

Since 1977, Davis has been a professor of music at the University of Wisconsin-Madison.

Richard The Saxophonist

American Saxophonist **Dick Stabile** formed his own orchestra in 1936 playing swing standards and ballads. He was noted for being an innovative and was the first bandleader to use more than three saxophones in a band. Sometimes he would use as many as five.

After the bombing of Pearl Harbour in 1941, Stabile enlisted in the US Navy and became a bandleader.

Returning to civilian life he was hired to work for Dean Martin and Jerry Lewis and appeared on the bill at their legendary Copacabana hotel run from 1950. He played with them until his death of heart failure in 1980.

Stabile is reputed to be the only man who could play the highest note on the sax, "a full octave above the top range of a saxophone".

Far Out Richard

American writer and folk singer **Richard Farina** emerged from the literary scene based around New Yorks' Greenwich Village in the early 1960s. He had already published short stories and poetry before being expelled from Cornell University.

After a whirlwind romance he married successful folk singer Carolyn Hester and he met the still unknown Bob Dylan, who played harmonica on her third album. The friendship between Dylan and Farina is the subject of the Pulitzer Prize winning book *Positively 4th Street* (2001) by David Hajdu.

In 1963 Farina made his first recording in London with fellow folk singer, Eric Von Schmidt. Dylan appears on the album, credited as Blind Boy Grunt. On this trip to Europe, Farina also met Joan Baez's sister, Mimi. The couple married on their return to the US and formed a folk music duo, releasing two albums in 1965.

His novel, *Been Down So Long It Looks Like Up To Me* (1966) is a counter-culture favourite.

Farina was killed in a motorcycle incident after celebrating his wife's 21st birthday in 1966.

His song, Birmingham Sunday, written about church bombings during the civil rights movement in Birmingham, Alabama, was recorded after his death by Joan Baez and used by director Spike Lee as the theme song to his documentary *4 Little Girls* (1997).

Behind The Scenes Richard

Son of arranger and conductor **Richard Maltby**, **Richard Maltby Jr.** is a successful American theatre director, screenwriter and producer. In 1978 he conceived and directed *Ain't Misbehavin'*, a musical review show intended as a tribute to the black American musicians of 1920s and 1930s Harlem. He won the Tony Award as that year's Best Director.

He also won the 1999 Best Director Tony Award for his work on musical Fosse. Maltby Jr. is credited as co-lyricist for *Miss Saigon* (1989).

He wrote the screenplay for *Miss Potter* (2006) the biopic about children's author Beatrix Potter, starring Rene Zellweger and Ewan McGregor.

There is every chance we have missed a Richard, or two.

Let us know at **www.stripepublishing.co.uk**

ACKNOWLEDGEMENTS

Thanks first of all to Dan Tester for the opportunity.

I am also grateful to Catherine English, who read the whole manuscript, made suggestions and patiently pointed out my grammatical shortcomings.

For encouragement and support, thanks go to my family and friends who helped with suggestions, so that discussions often became like talking about collections of rare objects; Michael and Julia Shanahan, Philip Shanahan, Mrs Audrie Mayes, Simon Thomas, Dominic and Ciara Elmidoro, Helen and Dorian Drake.

And finally, a major thank you to Stuart Tilbury for making the connection.

BIBLIOGRAPHY

Books

Britain Since 1945: The People's Peace.
Kenneth Morgan (Oxford) 2001

The Oxford History of Britain
Kenneth Morgan (Oxford) 1993

The Art Book
(London) 1999

The 20th Century Art Book (London) 1996

The Oxford Dictionary of Quotations (2nd Edition) (Oxford)
1964

Art of the Twentieth Century Vol I&II
Ingo Walker (Koln) 1998

RECOMMENDED WEBSITES

www.who2.com
www.allmusic.com
www.allmovie.com
www.bbc.co.uk
www.chortle.co.uk
www.cricinfo.com
www.imdb.com
www.jsc.nasa.gov
www.sporting-heroes.net
www.wikipedia.org
www.exclassics.com/newgate/ngintro.htm
www.trutv.com/library/crime/serial_killers
www.richardburton.com
www.richardiii.net
www.urbandictionary.com
business.timesonline.co.uk/tol/business/specials/rich_list
http://nobelprize.org/nobel_prizes/peace/laureates
http://improbable.com/ig/ – is an antidote to the Nobel
prize